CONTRACTS SIMULATIONS

by

Michael P. Malloy
Distinguished Professor and Scholar
University of the Pacific
McGeorge School of Law

Deborah R. Gerhardt
Associate Professor of Law
University of North Carolina
School of Law

BRIDGE TO PRACTICE®

WEST ACADEMIC PUBLISHING

Bridge to Practice Series is a trademark registered in the U.S. Patent and Trademark Office.

© 2015 LEG, Inc. d/b/a West Academic

    444 Cedar Street, Suite 700
    St. Paul, MN 55101
    1-877-888-1330

West, West Academic Publishing, and West Academic are trademarks of West Publishing Corporation, used under license.

Printed in the United States of America

ISBN: 978-0-314-28842-4

ACKNOWLEDGEMENTS

We gratefully acknowledge the following people whose assistance, support, and encouragement were so important to each of us:

Michael P. Malloy: I thank West Academic's Publisher Louis Higgins, acquisitions editor Bonnie Karlen, and the Bridge to Practice Series Editor, Professor Michael Vitiello, for the offer to work on this exciting project, and for their continuing support during its development.

The text of this book, and all the extrinsic evidence available, should make it clear that I owe a great deal to the resourcefulness and insights of my gifted co-author, Deborah R. Gerhardt. I am also grateful to my students over the years, especially my *Contracts* students, who have taught me more than I could have ever anticipated. I hope there was consideration on both sides. This project would have been impracticable for me, if not outright impossible, without the generous assistance of Janice Johnson, Director of the Pacific McGeorge Faculty Support Office, and all the talented members of her staff. I also thank Gerald M. Caplan, Joseph Perillo, Claude D. Rohwer and Anthony M. Skrocki, *emeriti et amici*, whose inquiring minds and thoughtfulness have always been an encouragement to me. I am their unintended beneficiary.

Finally, special thanks are due to my wife, Susie A. Malloy, who has an unerring eye for detail, and to my children, who served as my technical advisers on all things digital and graphic. They are, respectively, the condition precedent and the conditions subsequent to a happy life.

Deborah R. Gerhardt: I am grateful to West editors Pam Siege, Bonnie Karlen and Louis Higgins for welcoming me as a West author, introducing me to Michael P. Malloy, and encouraging us to embark on this project. Michael was the perfect coauthor – his expertise, creative spirit and clever sense of humor (even when a laptop was stolen or a hard drive crashed) made the bicoastal writing process gratifying and fun.

Many friends and colleagues offered comments and thoughtful feedback. I am especially grateful to Daniel Moore for generously permitting us to reproduce his contract and dynamic drawings for the Parol Evidence chapter. I owe many thanks to Paul Sandberg who shared with me fascinating practical insights about contracts in the film industry. I am grateful to Douglas Baird for his support and marvelous book, RECONSTRUCTING CONTRACTS. It is one of my most valued teaching resources. My first two 1L Contracts classes were intensely curious to know how the common law of contracts plays out in practice. Their thirst for this knowledge was a primary motivating force for this book. I am grateful to my students Max P. Biedermann, Carolyn R. Detmer, and Maddi Pfefferle who provided excellent research assistance.

The biggest share of my gratitude goes, as always, to my beloved husband Michael J. Gerhardt who motivates me to be better at everything I do. He introduced me to Douglas Baird and Paul Sandberg, provided thoughtful advice on several chapters and always enriches my life with loving support.

INTRODUCTION

————————

Most introductory law school contracts texts use judicial opinions, state statutes and restatements summarizing the law as primary instructional materials. Reading these sources is important if we are to understand the legal doctrine and how it is interpreted by courts when a business relationship falls apart. In those conflicts, judges interpret statutes, common law rules and agreements to discern whether an agreement amounts to a contract that the law will enforce. If it does, the court must then decide who wins, and what they get. But judicial opinions alone do not offer a complete picture of what it is like to work with contracts in the practice of law.

Because reading judicial opinions, statutes and restatements is so essential to understanding the law, some law students finish their first year contracts class without taking much time to critically examine real contracts. In some courses, students may not have a chance to examine even one! This book takes a different approach. Our purpose is to give students the opportunity to see how legal doctrine may be applied to actual written agreements. The primary materials for this course are contracts.

In this course, you will be encouraged to reconsider the terms in agreements. Think about how you could improve them to set forth the parties' intentions and obligations clearly. For example, if one party is supposed to pay another to work, will it be clear to both sides what the job is? Does the agreement identify what the service provider will be paid and when? If basic terms like these are not written clearly, the contract does not adequately lay out the terms of the relationship, and will increase the likelihood of a conflict. We encourage you to strive to write agreements that are so clear that the parties know what is expected of them. The best contracts are drafted after the difficult "what if" questions are asked and answered. In a well-structured relationship, the participants know their rights and obligations so the agreement can sit in a drawer, and there will be no need to engage lawyers and go to court. As you read through the agreements in each chapter, think critically about how you might avoid future disputes through better drafting from the beginning.

A well-written contract clearly defines a business relationship. It anticipates difficulties and states what will happen if they occur. If it does this job well, it is more likely to function as a practical guide for the parties and less likely to generate litigation. In each chapter, we present form contracts with the hope students will grow to understand that there is no such thing as a form that will work in every situation. We want this book to be a laboratory for experimentation where students feel free to mark up, delete and change terms that they find unclear or inapplicable to the situation.

We encourage you to begin this course by reflecting on your ideals for transactional writing. Bring in your apartment lease or the iTunes Terms of

Use. Go on line and find some contracts. Look at them together. What makes them work or not work? Think about what you can learn from reading these models. Consider beginning this course by drafting a list of aspirations and best practices for good contract drafting – not a bad place to begin a satisfying life in the law!

Michael P. Malloy
Deborah R. Gerhardt
April 2015

SUMMARY OF CONTENTS

———

TABLE OF CONTENTS

———————

CONTRACTS
SIMULATIONS

BRIDGE TO PRACTICE™

CHAPTER ONE

OFFER AND ACCEPTANCE

I. INTRODUCTION

Many modern contract disputes focus on the meaning of a contract, not whether a contract was formed in the first place. Sometimes, however, you may need to determine whether an enforceable agreement was made.[1] Other times you may need to pinpoint when an agreement was reached in order to identify what terms are part of the deal.[2] Identifying that critical moment can be challenging because contract negotiations are often fluid. The parties seeking to form a business relationship may not use the words "I offer" or "I accept." Therefore, if you understand the legal consequences of words and actions, you will be better prepared to provide effective counsel. This chapter will give you a chance to examine whether an enforceable contract has been entered and to determine its terms. You may also consider how you would advise each party to act and speak during negotiations to assure that all desired or necessary provisions are part of the deal before the parties reach a final agreement.

II. OVERVIEW OF THE LAW

Determining whether mutual assent occurred is an important threshold inquiry. What is mutual assent? One way to think of it is the sum of an offer and acceptance:

$$\text{offer} + \text{acceptance} = \text{mutual assent}[3]$$

If an offer is made and accepted, mutual assent exists.[4] There still may not be a valid contract for other reasons, but determining mutual assent remains an important step in determining whether an agreement was made and the content of its terms.[5] The Restate-

---

[1] *See Leonard v. Pepsico, Inc.*, 88 F. Supp. 2d 116 (1999) (considering whether response to television advertisement results in enforceable contract); *Maryland Supreme Corp. v. Blake Co.*, 279 Md. 531 (1979) (determining whether communications between general contractor and subcontractor were negotiations or resulted in enforceable agreement); *Marvin v. Marvin*, 18 Cal. 3d 660, 557 P.2d 106 (1976) (determining whether Michelle Marvin could enforce spoken promise to give her half of property Lee Marvin acquired during seven years she lived with him).

[2] *See Hill v. Gateway 2000, Inc.*, 105 F.3d 1147 (7th Cir. 1997) (holding that contract terms contained in box became enforceable after purchaser failed to return product within 30 days).

[3] *See* 1 SAMUEL WILLISTON & RICHARD A. LORD, A TREATISE ON THE LAW OF CONTRACTS § 3:4 (4th ed. 2014); *Lonergan v. Scolnick*, 276 P.2d 8 (1954) ("There can be no contract unless the minds of the parties have met and mutually agreed upon some specific thing. This is usually evidenced by one party making an offer which is accepted by the other party.").

[4] 1 WILLISTON & LORD, § 3:4.

[5] *Lucy v. Zehmer*, 84 S.E.2d 516 (1954); *Raffles v. Wichelhaus*, 159 Eng. Rep. 375 (1864); 1 WILLISTON & LORD, § 3:4 ("Invalidating causes—mistake, misapprehension, fraud, duress and

ment 2d of Contracts defines an offer as "the manifestation of willingness to enter into a bargain so made as to justify another person in understanding that his assent to that bargain is invited and will conclude it."[6] Acceptance of the offer occurs when the other party manifests "assent to the terms thereof made by the offeree in a manner invited or required by the offer"[7] These definitions require us to consider whether one party's communications are specific enough to form an offer and whether the other party has agreed to its terms. The words "manifest" in both definitions instruct us to use objective theory (explored in the next chapter) to examine the conduct and words of the parties and to ignore any secret unexpressed motives. Chapter two will give you an exercise to practice applying objective theory, but for now you can begin to reflect on how it may be used to establish default rules in contract law. It may also influence your decision to encourage your clients to speak up and state what they want when negotiating.[8]

III. THE CREAM IN MY COFFEE

To begin to understand how a combination of words or conduct may reveal when an offer and acceptance occur, let's start with a basic situation we all face. If I go to my neighborhood coffee shop and say, "I would like a cup of coffee." The clerk responds, "That will be $1.00." I hand her a one dollar bill. She hands me a cup of coffee. Did we just enter into a contract? If so, who made an offer? When was it accepted? Was a written document necessary for the contract to be formed? If the clerk prints a receipt that says I paid $10.00 instead of $1.00 does that effect the terms of the transaction? What does the $10.00 receipt teach us about writings that accompany agreements?

In the first coffee example, I spoke with the clerk. What if I didn't? Are words always necessary to create an offer or acceptance? My assent may be reflected in what I do, even if I say nothing.[9] Consider this variation on the coffee shop scenario. After ten weeks of buying the same $1 coffee five days a week, the clerk and I have gotten better acquainted. She knows I don't like to talk much before my first coffee. On Monday morning of the eleventh week of the semester, I put $1 on her counter, and she hands me a cup so I can serve myself coffee. Are we entering into a contract even though in my pre-coffee state I say nothing? If so, pinpoint the moments of offer and acceptance. Can silence amount to an acceptance?[10] Also consider whether our actions on that morning alone form our agreement or if other facts influenced your determination.[11]

Another important point to remember is that mutual assent cannot occur until an of-

---

undue influence, for example—can all, to the extent that they vitiate a party's assent to a bargain, have an effect on the agreement.").

[6] Rest. (2d) Contracts: Offer Defined § 24 (1981).

[7] Rest. (2d) Contracts: Acceptance of Offer Defined; Acceptance by Performance; Acceptance by Promise § 50 (1981).

[8] DOUGLAS G. BAIRD, RECONSTRUCTING CONTRACTS 20-24 (2013).

[9] *See* 2 WILLISTON & LORD, § 6:43.

[10] Rest. (2d) Contracts: Acceptance By Silence or Exercise of Dominion § 69(1) (1981) ("silence and inaction operate as an acceptance . . . only: (a) Where an offeree takes the benefit of offered services with reasonable opportunity to reject them and reason to know that they were offered with the expectation of compensation. (b) Where the offeror has . . . given the offeree reason to understand that assent may be manifested by silence or inaction, and the offeree . . . intends to accept the offer. (c) Where because of previous dealings . . . , it is reasonable that the offeree should notify the offeror if he does not intend to accept.")

[11] *Id.*

fer is accepted. A series of offers may or may not lead to acceptance of one of the proposed deals. We refer to a party making an offer as the "offeror," but that title is not fixed. A buyer and seller may trade offers so that the title "offeror" moves like a tossed ball from party to party until the negotiation ends.

The following example illustrates how the "offeror" status may switch as a buyer and seller negotiate. I am tired of having to spend $1,000 per year to fix a car with a blue book value of $1,500. Over coffee one morning at the neighborhood coffee shop, I offer to sell it to you for $1,200. Once my offer has been expressed, you may accept it. But I do not lose control of the situation entirely. I may still change my mind before you accept and revoke the offer. If we walk outside and you take a look at the car and see it needs new tires, you may reject my terms and propose a new deal. You may think the car is only worth $800. If you say, "I can't pay $1,200, but I would pay $800 for it," you have rejected my initial offer and have made a counter-offer. Now I can accept or change the terms again, making another counter-offer. Perhaps we will agree to a deal and form a contract—perhaps we will not.

Apply these concepts to the following problem. Alex Wiley got a green light from investors to produce a pilot for a television series, *Sugar and Cream*, a police procedural featuring two female officers going undercover in a local branch of the national Queequeg Coffee chain. Alex is considering casting an actor named Katie Fleming, whom he met in a graduate acting program. Alex has some concerns about hiring his friend for this job. Katie is immensely talented but has struggled with substance abuse. Alex called Katie to see how she is, and learned that after spending time at a top rehabilitation facility, she has been sober for six months.

Alex asked, "Katie, I'm interested in casting you as the lead in my new series. Are you free?"

Katie responded, "Seriously? I am free until next summer when I've committed to direct a youth Shakespeare production."

"We should be done with the pilot by then," Alex says. " I'm going to have our casting director set up a reading."

After the reading, Alex texted Katie,

UR in my friend. Who should get the paperwork?

Katie texted back,

Send it to my lawyer. Pavlov Dogg. p.dogg@DentArthurDent&Prefect.com.

Alex responded,

gr8 need you to turn it around by next week K?

Katie responded,

K   can do!

An hour later, Alex emailed copies of the following document to Pavlov and to Katie.

**TEST OPTION/PILOT/SERIES
PERFORMER AGREEMENT – PRINCIPAL TERMS**

DATE: August 7, 20__

PROGRAM: "Sugar and Cream" ("Program")

ARTIST: Katie Fleming

ROLE: Kay "Sugar" Kandu

LENDER:

These Test Option/Pilot/Series Services Agreement – Principal Terms ("Principal Terms") together with the Standard Terms attached hereto as Exhibit A (together, the "Agreement") set forth the agreement between <u>LLC ("Producer")</u>, and _____, f/s/o _____ (referred to herein as "Artist"), c/o _____.

1. <u>CONDITIONS PRECEDENT</u>. Producer's obligations under this Agreement are subject to:

1.1.   Producer's receipt of copies of this Agreement fully executed by Artist in each place indicated;

1.2.   Producer's receipt from Artist of a completed (to Producer's satisfaction) INS Form I-9 (Employment Eligibility Verification Form), and any visas, work permits and/or other documents determined by Producer to be necessary to establish Artist's eligibility to render services required under this Agreement;

1.3.   Producer's receipt of a copy of Lender's California Certificate of Registration, or other evidence (in form and substance satisfactory to Producer) that Lender is authorized to do business in California; and

1.4.   Producer entering into a fully executed agreement with _____ for the production of the Program.

2. GENERAL. Any engagement of Artist's services under this Agreement is subject to the terms of this Agreement, including, without limitation, terms applicable in the event of Artist's default, disability or death and the occurrence of an event of force majeure. Any engagement of Artist's services by Producer hereunder will be on a "pay or play" basis, such that Producer shall not be obligated to actually utilize the services of Artist for which Artist is engaged. As a general matter, Artist will be entitled to receive Artist's fees for any engagement under this Agreement only if and to the extent to which Artist actually renders the services for such engagement, provided, however, that if this Agreement provides that Artist is "confirmed for pay or play compensation" with respect to such engagement ("Confirmed for Pay or Play Compensation"), Producer will have an obligation to pay Artist for the services even if not utilized, provided that Artist was ready, willing and able to provide the services (subject to exception for an event of force majeure and related events as provided in the Standard Terms and subject to set off for any compensation received by Artist for professional services rendered that Artist would not have been able to render had Artist's services actually been utilized for such engagement). All services of Artist under this Agreement shall be subject to the supervision and control of Producer.

3. TEST/TEST DATE. In consideration of Producer agreeing to consider Artist for the Role in a one-hour pilot for the Program ("Pilot"), Artist will appear for such screen test(s) and/or reading(s) (the "Test") for the Role on such date, and at such time(s) and location(s) as Producer reasonably designates. The Test is currently scheduled for 9:00 AM, August 8, 20__ at _____**TBD**_____, which time, date, and location are subject to change.

4. PILOT OPTION/SERVICES/FEE.

4.1.   Pilot Option. In consideration of Producer agreeing to consider Artist for the Role, Artist grants to Producer the exclusive, independent and irrevocable option to engage Artist for the Role in the Pilot pursuant to the terms and conditions hereof (the "Pilot Option"). Producer will exercise the Pilot Option, if at all, by written notice to Artist on or before thirty-eight (38) business days following the Test.

4.2.   Pilot Services. If Producer exercises its Pilot Option, Artist agrees to render all services as a performer in the Role reasonably required by Producer in connection with the Pilot pursuant to all the terms and conditions of this Agreement. Artist's services in connection with the Pilot will commence on the date, and be rendered at the time(s) and location(s) as Producer designates and will continue through Artist's completion of all of Artist's services under this Agreement. Producer contemplates that principal photography of the Pilot shall commence on or about October 14, 20__, which date is subject to change by Producer. Producer contemplates exclusive pre-production services for Artist shall commence on or about October 2, 20__, which date is subject to change by Producer, provided that Artist shall be contractually available on October 2, 20__.

4.3.   __Pilot Fee__. Provided that Artist is not in material breach or default of this Agreement and completes Artist's Pilot services in the Role when and as required under this Agreement, Producer will pay to Artist a flat fee of Forty Thousand Dollars ($40,000) (the "Pilot Fee") for up to 8 pre-production days, up to 15 days principal photography days ("Pilot Shoot Days") and up to 5 post-production days for a total of 28 days and any travel time in connection therewith ("Pilot Days"). In the event Producer requires Artist to provide more days of service than the number of Pilot Days, Producer will pay to Artist a prorated day rate equal to the amount of the Pilot Fee divided by the number of Pilot Days. Artist shall become Confirmed for Pay or Play Compensation for the Pilot Fee upon Producer's exercise of the Pilot Option (if ever) and commencement of Artist's services on the Pilot.

5. __SERIES OPTIONS/SERVICES/FEES__. If Producer proceeds to production of a series based in whole or in part on the Pilot or the underlying material thereof ("Series") and Artist was engaged to provide services as a performer in the Role on the Pilot, Producer shall have an irrevocable option to engage Artist to render services in the Role for each Series Year (as defined below) as follows:

5.1.   __Series Options__.

5.1.1.   __First Series Year Option__. Producer shall have the option to engage Artist to render services in the Role for the first year of the Series ("First Series Year"), if at all, by written notice to Artist on or before the date that is 12 months after the date of completion of principal photography for the Pilot.

5.1.2.   __Second Series Year Option__. If Producer has exercised its option for Artist's services for the First Series Year, Producer shall have the irrevocable option to engage Artist to render services in the Role for the second year of the Series ("Second Series Year"), if at all, by written notice to Artist on or before the date that is the later of three months after the date of completion of principal photography for the First Series Year or the end of the First Series Year.

5.1.3.   __Third Through Sixth Series Years Options__. If Producer has exercised its option for Artist's services for the Second Series Year, Producer shall have irrevocable options to engage Artist for the Role for each of the third through sixth year of the Series (defined as the "Third", "Fourth", "Fifth", and "Sixth" "Series Year", respectively), if at all, by written notice to Artist on or before the date that is the later of three months after completion of principal photograph of the immediately preceding Series Year or the end of the immediately preceding Series Year.

5.2.   __Series Services__. Each "Series Year" shall be a period of 12 months from the date of exercise of the option for the applicable Series year. Artist agrees to render all services as a performer in the Role reasonably required by Producer in connection with each Series Year for which Producer exercises its option pursuant to all the terms and conditions hereof. Artist's services in connection with each Series Year will commence on such date, and be rendered at such time(s) and location(s) as Producer designates and will continue through end of the applicable Series Year. Notwithstanding anything in this Agreement to the contrary, in no event will Artist's services under this Agreement extend beyond the date that is seven (7) years from the date of Producer's exercise of the option for the First Series Year.

5.3. Series Fees. Provided that Artist is not in material breach or default of this Agreement and completes Artist's applicable Series services in the Role when and as required under this Agreement, Artist's fee ("Episode Fee") and the number of episodes for which Artist will be Confirmed for Pay or Play Compensation for the applicable Series Year are as follows:

Series Year	Episode Fee	# of Episodes Confirmed for Pay or Play Compensation
First Series Year	$40,000.00	All Produced
Second Series Year	$41,600.00	All Produced
Third Series Year	$43,264.00	All Produced
Fourth Series Year	$44,995.00	All Produced
Fifth Series Year	$46,794.00	All Produced
Sixth Series Year	$48,666.00	All Produced

For the purpose of the number of Episodes Confirmed for Pay or Play Compensation for the First Series Year, at Producer's election, the Pilot will be included as one (1) episode. Artist shall be Confirmed for Pay or Play Compensation for the applicable Episode Fee for the number of episodes set forth above as Episodes Confirmed for Pay or Play Compensation for the applicable Series Year upon Producer's exercise of the applicable option and commencement of Artist's services therefor.

6. SCREEN CREDIT. If Artist is not in material breach or default of this Agreement, subject to any applicable and binding collective bargaining agreements, Producer shall accord Artist screen credit, in the main titles or opening titles, at Producer's discretion, on the Pilot and each episode of the Series on which Artist renders and completes the applicable services indicated above with credit in the form of: "_____", in first position among Series regular cast. The above reference to "main titles" is to the credits, whether during, before or after each episode, where the "directed by" credit appears.

7. MISCONDUCT. If, in the opinion of ABC, Artist shall commit any act or do anything which might tend to bring Artist into public disrepute, contempt, scandal, or ridicule, or which might tend to reflect unfavorably on Producer, Producer's affiliates, any sponsor of a program created by Producer, any such sponsor's advertising agency, any network or stations broadcasting or scheduled to broadcast a program created by Producer, or any licensee of Producer, or to injure the success of any use of the Series or any program, Producer may, upon written notice to Artist, immediately terminate the Artist's employment hereunder. In the event Producer terminates Artist's services pursuant to the provisions of this Paragraph, Producer shall be discharged from all obligations hereunder by making any and all payments earned and payable on account of services performed by Artist prior to such date of termination. The guarantee, if any, applicable to the cycle in which such termination is effective shall be automatically reduced to the number of programs produced in such cycle and on which Artist rendered services prior to the effective date of such termination. In addition to whatever other right Producer may have, Producer may also remove Artist's credit, if any, from all such programs on which such credit may have appeared.

8.   <u>ADDITIONAL PROVISIONS</u>.

8.1.   <u>Dressing Room</u>. In connection with the Pilot and Series, Artist shall be provided with the exclusive use of one compartment in no less than a two-compartment trailer during all periods that Artist is providing principal photography services hereunder as required by Producer.

9.   <u>NO CONFLICTING OBLIGATIONS</u>. Artist represents and warrants that Artist does not have and will not enter into any obligations that might interfere with Artist's ability and availability to perform the services herein in accordance with Producer's requirements and schedule.

This Agreement represents the entire agreement between the parties and cannot be modified orally, and no other statements are relied on in executing this Agreement. This Agreement may be executed in two (2) or more counterparts each of which shall be deemed an original, but all of which taken together shall constitute one and the same instrument.

ACCEPTED AND AGREED: _____

By: _____

Name: _____

Title: _____

Date Signed: _____

Signed: _____

By: _____

Name: _____

Title: _____

Date Signed: _____

Questions

A. Before this document is signed, can you make an argument that either an offer or acceptance has been made? If so, pinpoint those moments. Do the definitions of "offer" and "acceptance" give you adequate tools to answer this question? What are the limits of these definitions? What additional rules would be helpful?

B. After reviewing the agreement, Katie says "I don't feel comfortable with paragraph 7."

    1. If you represent Katie, how would you respond?

    2. If you represent Alex, why would you want Paragraph 7 in this agreement?

    3. If Alex insists that Katie will not be hired without a "morals clause" in the contract, is a compromise possible? Is anything in the language of this "morals clause" especially problematic from Katie's perspective? If so, how would you recommend changing the language? What part of paragraph 7 would be most problematic for Katie? Would you recommend deleting or changing that language? How would you justify your suggested changes to opposing counsel?

C. Below are two alternative morals clauses that you may consider offering as substitutes. Would either of these provisions make sense as a possible substitute for paragraph 7?

Alternative 1

"If at any time, in the opinion of Producer, Artist becomes the subject of public disrepute, contempt, or scandal that affects Artist's image or goodwill, then Producer may, upon written notice to Artist, immediately suspend or terminate this Endorsement Agreement and Artist's services hereunder, in addition to any other rights and remedies that Producer may have hereunder or at law or in equity."

Alternative 2

"If at any time during the Term Artist is convicted of a felony or pleads guilty or 'no contest' to a felony, then Producer may, upon written notice to Artist, suspend or terminate this Agreement and Artist's services hereunder, in addition to any other rights and remedies that Producer may have hereunder or at law or in equity."

D. After Katie and Alex come to an agreement on Paragraph 7, Katie signs the document in your office. You scan it, save it as a pdf file, and email the document to Alex's counsel. Now revise your answer to Question No. 1. Is there an agreement *after* Katie signs the document but *before* it is signed by Alex?

E. For now, we are concerned with whether and when a contract is formed between

Katie and Alex. Are there other possible contract issues raised by the terms of the agreement that Alex sent to Pavlov and Katie? For future reference, you may want to prepare an informal agenda of these other issues, contrasting the likely positions of someone in Alex's position and someone in Katie's.

CHAPTER TWO

THE OBJECTIVE THEORY
OF CONTRACTS

I. INTRODUCTION

Lawyers are sometimes asked to review communications exchanged between people to determine whether a contract was formed. This chapter is designed to help you understand how to assess whether a contract was formed and how to interpret its terms using objective theory. You will be asked to review statements made by Donald Trump and the comedian Bill Maher and conclude whether these two men entered an enforceable contract. Before doing so, the next few paragraphs show you two approaches—one subjective and one objective – that have been used to analyze whether the parties entered an enforceable agreement.

II. OVERVIEW OF THE LAW

Objective theory has been the generally accepted approach to contract interpretation for over a century.[1] Early common law courts also applied this approach.[2] By the early nineteenth century, however, courts often looked at contract formation as a subjective question of whether the parties believed they had made a contract, or whether there had been a "meeting of the minds."[3] One problem in applying the subjective test is that one can never know for sure what another person is thinking. To apply the subjective standard, courts would have to set aside time and resources for a trial, empanel a jury and put witnesses on the stand to assess credibility, even if the circumstances made it seem outrageous that a reasonable person would believe that a contract was formed.

For this reason, modern courts generally apply objective theory to determine whether mutual assent occurred.[4] In doing so, courts ask whether the outward statements and con-

---

[1] *See* DOUGLAS G. BAIRD, RECONSTRUCTING CONTRACTS 16 (2013).

[2] *But cf.* Farnsworth, *"Meaning" in the Law of Contracts*, 76 Yale L.J. 939, 943-945 (1967) (arguing for early common law provenance for subjective theory).

[3] *See id.* at 945 ("[T]he metaphor [of the "meeting of the minds"] accorded well with the "will theory" of contracts, which attained hegemony in the nineteenth century"). On the history of the "subjective" or "will" theory and its eventual displacement by the objective theory, see MORTON J. HORWITZ, THE TRANSFORMATION OF AMERICAN LAW 1780-1860 180-188 (1977).

[4] For Judge Learned Hand's classic statement of the objective theory, see *Hotchkiss v. National City Bank*, 200 F. 287, 293 (S.D.N.Y. 1911) ("A contract has, strictly speaking, nothing to do with the personal, or individual, intent of the parties. A contract is an obligation attached by the mere force of law to certain acts of the parties, usually words, which ordinarily accompany and represent a known intent. If, however, it were proved by twenty bishops that either party, when he used the words, intended something else than the usual meaning which the law imposes upon them, he would still be held, unless there were some mutual mistake, or something else of the sort. Of course, if it appear by other words, or acts, of the parties, that they attribute a peculiar meaning to

duct of the parties can reasonably be interpreted to reflect a serious and concrete agreement.[5] Secret concerns or motives are not the focus of objective analysis.[6] Rather, courts examine the parties' statements, conduct and context.[7] As Professor Corbin famously wrote, "Parties are bound by the reasonable meaning of what they said and not by what they thought."[8]

Sometimes even if spoken words appear to support a finding that a contract was formed, the context may signal to a reasonable observer that neither party actually intended to form a contract. If the context or outward conduct of the parties makes it clear that neither intended a contract to be formed, there is no manifestation of mutual assent.[9] For example, as a classroom hypothetical your professor may say, "I offer to sell you a new car (valued at $25,000) for $1000 if you agree to drive my three boys to music lessons for two years. Tell me whether you accept my offer." A student raises his hand and responds, "I accept." Even though the spoken words sound like a contract, the context makes it clear that the discussion involved a classroom hypothetical, not a genuine offer.

Subjective understandings are not entirely ignored even under objective theory.[10] If the party who tries to enforce a contract knows the defendant's statement is a joke and not a serious offer, then he cannot prevail in establishing a contract was formed. For example, in *Leonard v. Pepsico*,[11] John Leonard claimed that a television advertisement featuring a teenager who trades in 7 million "Pepsi points" for a Harrier Jet–and who arrives at school in the jet–was an offer that he could (and did) accept by accumulating and delivering 7 million points to Pepsico. If Leonard knew that Pepsi's ad was a joke and that the company did not seriously intend to offer military jets in exchange for Pepsi points, objective theory would not permit him to establish that a contract was made.[12]

---

such words as they use in the contract, that meaning will prevail, but only by virtue of the other words, and not because of their unexpressed intent.").

[5] *See, e.g., Leonard v Pepsico, Inc.*, 88 F.Supp.2d 116, 127 (S.D.N.Y. 1999) ("In evaluating the commercial [as an offer or not], the Court must not consider defendant's subjective intent in making the commercial, or plaintiff's subjective view of what the commercial offered, but what an objective, reasonable person would have understood the commercial to convey."), *affirmed per curiam,* 210 F.3d 88 (2d Cir. 2000); *Lucy v. Zehmer,* 196 Va. 493, 84 S.E.2d 516, 518, 520 (1954) (enforcing contract for sale of farm; rejecting seller's claim that "he . . . considered that the offer was made in jest" and that he was "high as a Georgia pine").

[6] *Cf. Oswald v. Allen*, 417 F.2d 43, 45 (2d Cir. 1969) (rejecting purported buyer's subjective understanding of the meaning of "Swiss Coin Collection," which was subject of contract of sale).

[7] *See Brant v. California Dairies*, 4 Cal.2d 128, 133, 48 P.2d 13, 16 (1935) (holding that undisclosed intentions of parties are, in absence of mistake, fraud, or similar grounds, immaterial; outward manifestation or expression of assent is controlling).

[8] Arthur L. Corbin, *Offer and Acceptance, and Some of the Resulting Legal Relations*, 26 Yale L. J. 204-6 (1917).

[9] *Cf. Kind v. Clark*, 161 F.2d 36 (2d Cir. 1947), *cert. denied*, 332 U.S. 808, 68 S.Ct. 108, 92 L.Ed. 385 (holding that parties intending fictitious transfer of stock does not result in enforceable contract for sale of stock).

[10] *See, e.g.*, Rest. (2d) Contracts: Effect of Misunderstanding § 20(2) (1981):

> The manifestations of the parties are operative in accordance with the meaning attached to them by one of the parties if
> (a) that party does not know of any different meaning attached by the other, and the other knows the meaning attached by the first party; or
> (b) that party has no reason to know of any different meaning attached by the other, and the other has reason to know the meaning attached by the first party.

[11] 88 F.Supp.2d 116 (S.D.N.Y. 1999), *affirmed per curiam*, 210 F.3d 88 (2d Cir. 2000).

[12] *Leonard*, 88 F.Supp.2d at 127.

III. THE JOKER IS WILD

Apply objective theory to explain how the following dispute should be resolved. During the 2012 presidential election, Donald Trump had launched a media campaign dedicated to proving that President Barack Obama was not born in the United States. Ostensibly, Trump was motivated to defend Article II, Section 1 of the United States Constitution, which requires a President to be a natural born citizen. After President Obama produced his birth certificate establishing that he was in fact born in the USA, Trump did not relent, demanding to see Obama's college records. (Trump suspected that Obama said something different about his place of birth when he applied to college.) To prompt Obama to release the records, Trump offered to give $5 million to a charity of President Obama's choice if he would release his college transcript.

Bill Maher is a political comedian who hosts an HBO talk show called *Real Time with Bill Maher*. While Trump was challenging the President's eligibility to hold the nation's highest executive office, Maher was scheduled to be a guest on the NBC television program, *The Tonight Show*. One of Bill Maher's writers proposed making a joke comparing the color of Trump's hair to that of an orangutan and suggested that orangutans and Trump are the only two life forms known to man with that hair color. Maher suggested upping the ante on the joke and linking it to the demands Trump made of Obama. Maher thought it would be fun to offer Trump $5 million if he could prove that he is not the son of his mother and an orangutan.

During his appearance on *The Tonight Show* with the host Jay Leno, Maher said, "Trump's on my case. He's not happy with me since I explained on Real Time he must be the spawn of his mother and an orangutan. Nothing else explains that hair color." He also said, "If Trump can come up with proof that he his not the child of his mother and an orangutan, I'm willing to offer Trump $5 million. . . ."

"Whoa!" Leno interjected. " Seriously? $5 million?"

Maher responded, "I'm willing to offer $5 million that Trump may give to a charity of his choice – Hair Club for Men, the Institute for Incorrigible Douche-baggery, whatever . . ."

On the morning after his appearance on *The Tonight Show*, Maher received the following letter from Trump's attorney:

Via Hand Delivery

Dear Mr. Maher,

I represent Donald J. Trump. On his behalf, I am writing to accept your offer made during the Jay Leno show to give Mr. Trump 5 million dollars if he can prove he is not the spawn of his mother and an orangutan.

Attached to this letter is a certified copy of Mr. Trump's birth certificate, showing that he is the son of Fred Trump, not an orangutan. Please remit 5 million dollars to Mr. Trump at your earliest convenience. The money will be divided equally among the following charities: March of Dimes, Hurricane Victims Fund, The Police Athletic League, The American Cancer Society and the Dana-Farber Cancer Institute.

Sincerely yours,

/s/

Scott S. Balber

Enclosure

Reportedly, when asked whether the bit about the orangutan was just a parody and not a contract, Trump responded, "That was venom. That wasn't a joke."

When Maher did not respond to the demand for $5 million, Trump's counsel filed a breach of contract suit in state court. Although he never responded directly to the letter from Trump's lawyer, Maher did tell his television audience that "Donald Trump must learn two things: what a joke is and what a contract is."

Questions

A. You are legal counsel for HBO. Assume that, before the NBC show was aired, you are brought in to approve the *Real Time* script that includes the orangutan statements. Please advise the HBO producers about (1) the risk of litigation from Trump based on the orangutan statements; (2) whether the statements as planned may be considered an offer to enter into a legally enforceable contract; and, (3) whether you would recommend making any changes in the script. [13]

B. Assume that you are clerking for the judge who is holding a status conference in the case *Trump v. Maher et al.* Advise the judge whether she should dismiss the breach of contract claim for failure to state a claim upon which relief can be granted.

C. Does your answer to Question B change if you apply the subjective theory of contract?

D. What if Trump had put $5 million in escrow when he made the offer to Obama?

---

[13] Please note that nobody else in the conference room apparently cares whether you think the orangutan statements are funny or not.

CHAPTER THREE

CONSIDERATION

I. INTRODUCTION

No legal system recognizes all promises as enforceable obligations. Contract doctrine separates out some promises the law will enforce from others that remain outside its reach. Consideration is one doctrine that serves as a dividing line. In the United States, promises are enforceable only if supported by consideration or, less frequently, a consideration substitute. You can think of the basic elements to a contract as:

Offer + Acceptance + Consideration = Contract

Sometimes detrimental reliance may substitute for consideration, but that is not the typical situation. The absence of consideration is one reason a promise may not be enforced. Other reasons exist as well. For example, a contract may not be enforceable if the subject matter violates public policy, if one party did not have the capacity to enter into the agreement or if the party was under duress and could not fairly bargain. You will have an opportunity to explore these possibilities in later chapters. For now, let's focus on the consideration piece of the basic formula.

II. OVERVIEW OF THE LAW

What is consideration? It is defined in terms of bargaining. The Restatement 2d of Contracts provides that "[t]o constitute consideration, a performance or a return promise must be bargained for."[1] How do we know that a bargain occurred? The Restatement tells us to look to see "if it is sought by the promisor in exchange for his promise and is given by the promisee in exchange for that promise."[2] Consideration can exist in the form of virtually anything valuable enough to make someone want to bargain for it.[3] Some common forms include a promise, money, an action, forbearance, or the "creation, modification, or destruction of a legal relation."[4]

This abstract definition becomes clearer if we look at concrete examples. Consider whether the following promises are "supported by consideration." Your alma mater has identified Isaiah as a top candidate among its applicant pool and has decided to offer him a four-year college scholarship. If the University would like Isaiah to commit to attend-

---

[1] Rest. (2d) Contracts: Requirement of Exchange; Types of Exchange § 71(1) (1981).

[2] *Id.* § 71(2).

[3] E. ALLAN FARNSWORTH, CONTRACTS § 2.2, at 48 (4th ed. 2004).

[4] Rest. (2d) Contracts: Requirement of Exchange; Types of Exchange § 71(2) (1981). *Reed v. University of North Dakota*, 589 N.W.2d 880 (N.D. 1999) (giving Reed a position as a participant in a race found to constitute consideration); Hamer v. Sidway, 27 N.E. 256 (N.Y. 1891) (providing classic example of forbearance).

ing, how could it structure the award in a way that would create a contract supported by consideration? Consider the following possibilities.

    a.   The University promises to award Isaiah a four-year scholarship.

    b.   The University promises to award Isaiah a four-year scholarship when he graduates from high school.

    c.   The University promises to award Isaiah a four-year scholarship if he promises to attend beginning in the fall of the following academic year.

    d.   The University promises to award Isaiah a four-year scholarship if he agrees to withdraw applications from all other schools to which he applied.

In each of these examples, the University makes the same promise: to award Isaiah a four-year scholarship. The difference in these examples lies in what–if anything—the University asks Isaiah to promise or do in return. Not all of them seek something *in exchange* for the scholarship.

The first example looks like a gift or the award of a prize. Without any additional facts, we cannot conclude that the promise is supported by consideration.[5] What about the second promise? It is not a sure thing. Isaiah must graduate from high school to get the scholarship, but the promise is not bargained in exchange for his agreement to do so. This second example is really a promise to give a gift that is conditioned on his graduation from high school, but the facts do not show any bargain. Isaiah may get this scholarship as soon as he graduates, but because the University did not seek anything from him in exchange for the award, the facts do not show that the University's promise was supported by consideration.[6] The third example offers the scholarship *in exchange* for his promise to attend in the next academic year. Isaiah's promise to attend is consideration for the school's promise to award the scholarship.[7] Similarly, in the fourth example, Isaiah's action of withdrawing applications from other schools is sought *in exchange* for the promised scholarship, and therefore this act, if taken, would constitute consideration.[8] Which of the four options would put Isaiah in the strongest position for securing the scholarship? If you represent the University and know that they are uncertain how much funding they will have for scholarships next year, which options would be best for your client? How would you advise them to proceed?

III. BABIES' BREATH

Apply these principles to the following examples to determine whether the promises at issue are supported by consideration.

---

[5] *See, e.g., Stonestreet v. Southern Oil Co.*, 37 S.E.2d 676 (N.C. 1946) (holding gratuitous promise of reimbursement unenforceable).

[6] *Cf. Jones v. Wichita State University,* 698 F.2d 1082 (10th Cir. 1983) (discussing academic conditions for college athletic scholarship).

[7] *See Alabama Football, Inc. v. Wright,* 452 F.Supp. 182 (N.D. Tex. 1977) (rejecting defunct football team's claim to recover signing bonus paid at time player signed agreement).

[8] See. *Hamer v. Sidway, supra* (holding that forbearance sought for by promisor is detriment to promisee sufficient to constitute consideration).

Dr. Maya Raudales is a pediatrician, research scientist and the founder of Angel Labs in Seattle, Washington. Maya became internationally famous for developing a unique product line of software and ventilators that help premature babies breathe and monitor their needs. Sometimes, a premature infant's lungs are so underdeveloped, the baby cannot survive outside a hospital's intensive care unit. Maya's company, Angel Labs, creates and sells ventilators. These breathing machines deliver warmed and humidified air directly into a baby's lungs until the infant develops the capacity to breathe on its own. The Angel Labs software is designed to monitor an infant's heart rate, the rate of oxygen delivery, air pressure and number of breaths per minute. The software collects and delivers the information so that the data can be used to advance research in medical science.

In 2007, Joe Bradley interviewed for a job with Angel Labs. At the interview, Maya explained that due to legal requirements, the company must keep its hospital patient information confidential. Maya told Joe, "I only hire people who promise to keep our customer history information secret. Will you do that?" Joe said, "Yes."

Joe began working for Angel Labs one month after graduating from Cal Tech's engineering school. He quickly became the company's top software developer. As part of his job, Joe had full access to Angel Labs' customer history information. For more than ten years, Maya has collected and studied the customer data. It contains information about each hospital's technology needs, private patient information and sales information. So that customer relations will not be lost if sales representatives leave or change their territory, the company gathers personal information about lead doctors, administrators and anyone else who makes decisions about purchasing hospital equipment. This information includes birthdays, hobbies, food preferences and sports loyalties. Angel Labs maintains this information in strict confidence, so that it can provide more personalized service than its competitors. Angel's excellent service has contributed substantially to its success.

In 2011 Angel Labs was paying Joe $100,000 per year. To reward him for his contributions and ensure he would stay with the company, Maya decided to offer him a written contract so that he would have job security for at least five years. Maya explained that she wanted Joe to lead a team to advance Angel Labs' ventilator monitoring software. The agreement contains the provisions excerpted below. After reviewing these provisions, address the questions that follow.

---

9. Angel Labs will pay Employee an annual salary of $100,000 per year. At the end of each calendar year, Angel Labs will pay Employee an additional $50,000 if the research and software development goals for the prior year were achieved.

10. Employee promises and covenants that while this agreement is in effect and for a period of two years after the termination of employment, Employee will not engage, directly or indirectly, as principal, agent, employer, employee, or in any capacity whatsoever in any software development business within the United States.

11. Employee will keep in strict confidence the Customer History Information and will not, at any time during his employment or afterwards, use the Customer History Information except for the purpose of performing his duties for Angel Labs. Employee acknowledges that Angel Labs maintains its Customer History Information secretly and that it is the sole property of Angel Labs. Employee promises to return all Customer History Information to Angel Labs immediately upon termination of his employment.

12. Employee acknowledges that he will be hired for a research project that is scheduled to last for five years, and that if he terminates his employment before the end of the five-year term, it will take Angel Labs at least one year to find and train a new project manager. Therefore, Employee will agree to pay $100,000 to Angel Labs if he terminates his employment before the end of the five-year term.

Questions

A. Analyze whether Joe had a contract with Angel Labs in the first years of his employment. If so, what were the promises made by each party? Was each party's promise supported by consideration?

B. Analyze whether the promises in the written contract are supported by consideration.

C. Assume that federal law requires nondisclosure of private medical information and that state unfair competition law and "trade secret" protection statutes provide remedies for companies if employees misuse confidential information or trade secrets. Given that these laws exist, does that change your answer to the previous question? Why did Maya's lawyer include paragraph 11 in Joe's employment agreement?

CHAPTER FOUR

CAPACITY

I. INTRODUCTION

Not every agreement has the force of law. The law of contracts governs a subset of agreements society has chosen to make enforceable.[1] When an agreement is enforceable, a party who was harmed by a breach may be entitled to damages, specific performance, or an injunction.[2] For public policy reasons, legislatures or courts carve out some categories of agreements that courts will not enforce. Some agreements are automatically put in the unenforceable set because of their subject matter.[3] Courts will not enforce contracts if the obligations created by it are illegal.[4] For example, courts will not help a hoodlum collect on his promise to commit a murder for $10,000. The illegal subject matter would make the contract void.[5] What does "void" mean? A void agreement creates no legal obligations.[6] These agreements are sometimes described as violating public policy, and they will not be enforced no matter who entered them.[7] Policymakers have decided that courts will not validate this group of agreements by acknowledging their validity and providing a remedy for a breach. The group of agreements that fit in this category varies from state to state.[8]

Sometimes the agreement must observe specific legal formalities to be considered enforceable. For example, a state legislature may enact a law stating that all real estate transactions must be written down and signed by both parties. These laws—requiring that the terms of the contract are written and signed—are called "statutes of frauds."[9] If a real estate transaction does not follow those formalities, it will generally be treated as unenforceable.[10]

---

[1] *See* 1 SAMUEL WILLISTON & RICHARD A. LORD, A TREATISE ON THE LAW OF CONTRACTS § 1:1 (4th ed. 2014).

[2] JOSEPH M. PERILLO, CONTRACTS § 1.8, at 19 (7th ed. 2014).

[3] Restatement (Second) of Contracts: Unenforceable Contracts § 8 cmt. b (1981) ("Some contracts are unenforceable because they arise out of illegal bargains").

[4] R.R. v. M.H., 426 Mass. 501, 689 N.E.2d 790 (1998) (contracts to sell children are illegal).

[5] Restatement (Second) of Contracts: Exchange of Promise for Performance § 72 cmt. d (1981).

[6] *See id.*

[7] *See* 5 SAMUEL WILLISTON & RICHARD A. LORD, A TREATISE ON THE LAW OF CONTRACTS § 12:1 (4th ed. 2014).

[8] For example, a contract that prohibits an employee from competing with her employer after she leaves her job that is unenforceable under California law may be enforced in the laws of many other states. *See e.g.,* Estee Lauder Companies Inc. v. Batra, 430 F. Supp. 2d 158, 177 (S.D.N.Y. 2006) (holding that although California has a fundamental policy against the enforcement of non-compete agreements, the agreement is enforceable under New York law).

[9] *See* 9 SAMUEL WILLISTON & RICHARD A. LORD, A TREATISE ON THE LAW OF CONTRACTS § 21:4 (4th ed. 2014).

[10] *See* 1 SAMUEL WILLISTON & RICHARD A. LORD, A TREATISE ON THE LAW OF CONTRACTS § 1:21 (4th ed. 2014).

Even if a document looks like a valid agreement, the context in which it was entered may create good reasons not to enforce it. As we studied earlier, mutual assent is essential to the formation of a contract. One party may have a cognitive impairment that prevents him or her from making a serious promise. Sometimes the impairment will be very temporary, like intoxication, and sometimes it will be long term, as when a person suffers from severe dementia. These, among other conditions, involve issues of capacity to enter into a contract.

II. OVERVIEW OF THE LAW

Incapacity of one or both parties to an agreeement may render the entire agreement void.[11] Another possibility is that the context may give one or both parties the option of treating the contract as void.[12] When such an option exists, the contract is "voidable."[13]

If one party is incapable of making an offer or accepting someone else's, mutual assent cannot occur because one of the two required elements (offer + acceptance) is missing. How do we test a person's capacity? One leading treatise summarizes the common law test as follows: "[i]ncapacity exists where a party does not understand the nature and consequences of what is happening at the time of the transaction."[14] Incapacity may result from age, mental impairment, intoxication, or other circumstances.[15]

Traditionally, youth–sometimes referred to as "minority"[16]–was enough to establish incompetence. At common law, the age of majority was 21.[17] Most states have lowered the age to 18.[18] At common law, a minor was not thought to have the capacity to enter an adult contract.[19]

At common law, courts often treated contracts entered into by incompetent persons as automatically void.[20] The more modern approach is to treat them as voidable by the incompetent person.[21] The purpose of the rule is to protect children from "squandering their wealth through improvident contracts with crafty adults who would take advantage

---

[11] Rest. (2d) § 12(1) (1981).

[12] See 1 SAMUEL WILLISTON & RICHARD A. LORD, A TREATISE ON THE LAW OF CONTRACTS § 1:20 (4th ed. 2014).

[13] See id. ("A voidable contract is one where one or more parties have the power, by a manifestation of election to do so, to avoid the legal relations created by the contract, or by ratification of the contract to extinguish the power of avoidance.").

[14] JOSEPH M. PERILLO, CONTRACTS § 8.9, at 276 (7th ed. 2014).

[15] See Restatement (Second) of Contracts §§ 14, 16 (1981).

[16] The Restatement refers to the incapacity category of youth as being "an infant." Id. § 12(2)(b). It doesn't mean gugu-gaga, just that the person is below a legally recognized minimum age of majority, typically as identifed by state statute. For discussion of incapacity due to youth, see W. Navin, The Contracts of Minors Viewed from the Perspective of Fair Exchange, 50 N.C.L.Rev. 517 (1972).

[17] Restatement (Second) of Contracts: Infants §14, cmt. a (1981).

[18] See Restatement (Second) of Contracts: Infants §14 (1981)("Unless a statute provides otherwise, a natural person has the capacity to incur only voidable contractual duties until the beginning of the day before the person's eighteenth birthday.").

[19] See Restatement (Second) of Contracts: Infants §14 cmt. a (1981).

[20] An incompetent person "has the power to void the contract entirely." Hauer v. Union State Bank of Wautoma, 192 Wis. 2d 576, 588, 532 N.W.2d 456, 460 (Ct. App. 1995).

[21] See 25 SAMUEL WILLISTON & RICHARD A. LORD, A TREATISE ON THE LAW OF CONTRACTS § 67:27 (4th ed. 2014).

of them in the marketplace."[22]

Consider the consequences of this rule. It has the advantage of clarity so that courts need not hold trials on whether young people meet the capacity test. But it has disadvantages as well. Not all children have bad judgment. One consequence of treating all minors as incompetent is that it may discourage adults from doing business with young persons who would like to participate in business deals.[23]

What are the practical effects of the rule? Does it make sense for some transactions but not others? Is it necessary to protect teenagers from purchasing used cars? Should social media services like Facebook, Twitter, and Instagram bar users who are younger than 18? If a fifteen year-old designs software and uses the money he earned to buy a car, are either of these transactions enforceable contracts? If a 17 year-old athlete is staying in a hotel room with his teammates, can the hotel collect payment for movies and wifi service that he orders? The facts set forth below give you the opportunity to see how this rule works in another common setting.

III. SENIORS WHO ARE MINORS

The Academy School wants to create a sense of team spirit among their senior class. Before the year begins, the school is taking the class on a mountain trip where they will experience a series of adventures together. The Academy plans to take the students hiking, rock climbing, spelunking and mountain biking. The final event will be dropping into a deep gorge on a zip line. The school plans to bring 120 students, all of whom will be starting their senior year, to Green River Valley Zip Line for what promises to be an unforgettable experience. On its website, Green River Valley Zip Line posts a form, a copy of which appears on the following pages.

A Green River Valley Zipline representative told the Academy about the waiver before the trip, but many of the students did not sign it. When they arrived at the park, a Green River employee gave copies to one of the chaperones for each student to sign.

---

[22] Halbman v. Lemke, 99 Wis. 2d 241, 245, 298 N.W.2d 562, 564 (1980).

[23] Vendors may be unwilling to deal with minors because innocence on the part of the vendor may not defend the vendor. *See id* at 28, 298 N.W.2d at 566. ("The infancy doctrine is designed to protect the minor, sometimes at the expense of an innocent vendor").

GREEN RIVER VALLEY ZIP LINE

RELEASE AND WAIVER FROM LIABILITY

Read Carefully Before Signing

I, _____, residing at _____, hereby
         (NAME)   (CITY, STATE)
acknowledge that I have voluntarily agreed to participate in the Green River Valley Zip Line located at Green River Valley Farm in Brevard, North Carolina (herein referred to as "Green River Valley Zip Line "), on _____, 20___, and I understand and assume all risks associated with zip line activities.

Age: _____ Height: _____ Gender M__ F__ Weight: _____
Notice: (Age 10) 70lbs Minimum 250lbs Maximum

For the valuable consideration of being permitted to participate in the Green River Valley Zip Line, I and each of my heirs, personal representatives, guardians, conservators, agents, successors and assigns, HEREBY RELEASE AND HOLD HARMLESS the following persons and entities (these entities are collectively referred to herein as "the Company"): (1) Green River Valley Zip Line and its owner and operator, Green River Valley, Inc., a North Carolina corporation, and its shareholders, officers, owners, employees, insurers, agents, volunteers, successors and assigns, and any of their subsidiaries, respective members, shareholders, directors, officers, and related persons and entities, in their official and individual capacities; (2) City of Brevard, and its employees and agents; and (3) the landowner who leases the property to Green River Valley, Inc. I specifically release these entities from any and all liability, claims, demands, actions, causes of action (including but not limited to negligence), claims of relief, or injuries related to or arising from my being a participant in the Green River Valley Zip Line or my presence at the Company's facilities. I, and each of my heirs, personal representatives, guardians, agents, conservators, successors and assigns, agree: a) not to make a claim against or sue the Company or attach property of the Company; b) to waive any and all claims against the Company; and c) to defend, indemnify, and hold harmless the Company for injury, death, or property damage caused by, resulting from or in any way related to my being a participant in the Green River Valley Zip Line or otherwise resulting from my presence at the Company's facility, whether or not such injury, death, or property damage was caused by the negligence of the Company or Company's staff. In the event I, or a representative on my behalf, take any legal action against the Company that is contrary to the terms of this Release, I agree to be responsible for all attorney fees and costs the Company incurs in defending such legal action, including any ultimate verdict or settlement.

I HAVE CAREFULLY READ THIS RELEASE AND FULLY UNDERSTAND ITS CONTENTS. I am aware that:

♦ Risk of injury from the activity and equipment utilized is significant, with the potential for permanent disability and death.
♦ Body parts, including hair, could become entangled in equipment, causing injury, pain, and disfigurement;
♦ I may fall from a height as high as 100 feet, resulting in severe injuries or death;
♦ I may slam into a platform or landing area, or miss the platform, resulting in injury and/or events leading to injury or death;
♦ I may not be securely fastened by a guide or employee and may fall, resulting in injury or death;
♦ Equipment could fail; cables may slip and/or break; harnesses could slip or break, resulting in injury or death;
♦ I may collide with another participant or employee, which may result in risks of death, paralysis, or serious injury;
♦ I may re-injure a previous injury;
♦ This is an outdoor activity and therefore includes risks associated with exposure to the elements, wild animals and insects, as well as heat exhaustion, hypothermia, and related conditions; the facility is located in a remote area without medical facilities, and delay may occur in treating health conditions;
♦ I may become sick from the swinging motion resulting in nausea, vomiting, dizziness, or other illness, and such condition may decrease reaction time resulting in injury.

This list is provided for illustrative and informative purposes only and is not intended to be exhaustive or to in any manner limit the intended broad reach of this release. This agreement is governed by the laws of the State of North Carolina; if any provision is held invalid, it is agreed that the remaining provisions shall remain in full force and effect.

I AM AWARE OF THE INHERENT AND OTHER RISKS ASSOCIATED WITH ZIP ACTIVITIES AND I UNDERSTAND THAT BY PARTICPATING IN THE GREEN RIVER VALLEY ZIP LINE, I ASSUME FULL RESPONSIBILITY FOR AND RISK OF BODILY INJURY, DEATH, OR PROPERTY DAMAGE, AND I EXPRESSLY AGREE THAT THE ABOVE RELEASE, WAIVER AND INDEMNITY AGREEMENT IS INTENDED TO BE AS BROAD AND INCLUSIVE AS POSSIBLE. I UNDERSTAND THAT I MAY CHOOSE NOT TO PARTICIPATE IN THE GREEN RIVER VALLEY ZIP LINE, AND IN SUCH CASE, I WILL IMMEDIATELY NOTIFY THE STAFF OF MY DECISION AND I WILL RECEIVE A REFUND AND WILL BECOME A DAY GUEST AT THE DAY GUEST RATE. I HAVE READ THIS RELASE OF LIABILITY AGREEMENT AND I UNDERSTAND THAT I AM GIVING UP LEGAL RIGHTS BY SIGNING IT, AND I AM FREELY AND VOLUNTARILY SIGNING IT WITHOUT ANY INDUCMENT.

Photo Release: I agree to allow this organization to photograph or videotape my participation in the course. I understand that the pictures may be used in promoting the organization.

DATE: _____, 20_____   _____
                                  City, State, Zip Code

                                  _____
                                  Email

                                  _____
                                  Signature

                                  _____
                                  Print Name

Questions

A. Zahr (a senior) bumped her head while climbing up to the Zipline platform before her first jump.

The Green River coach asked her, "Are you ok?"

Zahr responded, "I think so—I'm dizzy."

"Do you still want to jump?"

Zahr did not want to look like a coward by climbing back down the ladder, and she was looking forward to this so much for weeks! She replied, "Ok."

Two days later, Zahr was feeling so ill that her parents took her to the emergency room, where she was examined. The doctor on call said she had a serious concussion, and the jumping likely made her injury worse. Because her family had no health insurance, her medical expenses amounted to $6,800.

Does the fact that the waiver is posted on the website bar Zahr or her parents from bringing a claim against Green River Zipline for her medical expenses?

B. Does it matter whether Zahr signed the agreement before or after she hit her head? Before or after she jumped?

C. If you represented Zahr, what other facts would you need to know before concluding whether she has a valid claim against Green River Zipline for her medical expenses?

D. If Zahr is already 18, can you make any other argument why this agreement should not be enforced?

E. You represent Green River Valley, Inc., the owner and operator of Green River Valley Zip Line, and it has asked you to review the waiver form. Would you recommend making any changes? If so, please mark it up and write a letter explaining your revisions.

CHAPTER FIVE

UNILATERAL CONTRACT

I. INTRODUCTION

Agreements that are formed by one party offering a promise in return for an action, *not* a return promise, are referred to as "unilateral contracts." You might respond by asking, "So what?" This is actually a very insightful response. We can classify contracts in all sorts of ways – contracts that are about cows, contracts that last for more than one year, contracts that are green – but not all of these classifications are *legally* significant categories. This simulation seeks to illustrate the legal significance of identifying an agreement as a *unilateral contract*.

Traditionally, discussion of unilateral contracts begins with what may seem like a bad joke. One guy says to another, "If you walk across the Southwark Bridge, I'll give you a ticket to tonight's performance of *The Merchant of Venice* at the Shakespeare's Globe Theatre." The second guy starts walking across the bridge. When he is half-way across, the first guy rides by in a hansom cab and shouts out, "I revoke my offer!" And so, the commentators used to tell us, there is no contract, because by the terms of the offer, only performance of the desired action would constitute acceptance, and the offer was revoked before it could be accepted.[1]

It may be that the law of unilateral contracts has become less treacherous over time. We still need to explore, however, how this doctrine works in practical terms. We should try to anticipate whether there might be a risk of the doctrine upsetting our client's expectations, and try to draft around it.

---

[1] *See, e.g.*, I. Maurice Wormser, *The True Conception of Unilateral Contracts*, 26 YALE L.J. 136 (1916). Almost 35 years later, Wormser finally repudiated this view of revocation of an offer seeking acceptance by performance. I. Maurice Wormser, *Book Review*, 3 J. LEG. ED. 145, 146 (1950) (stating "I have repented, so that now, clad in sackcloth, I state frankly, that my point of view has changed").

II. OVERVIEW OF THE LAW

Offers typically invite acceptance in any reasonable manner, although the offeror has the power to require a particular mode of acceptance.[2] Where the terms of the offer do not clearly resolve the question of the mode of acceptance, the offeree is free to choose acceptance by promising or by rendering a requested performance.[3] However, if offeror specifies acceptance by performance of some action, *i.e.*, looking towards a unilateral contract, then we have to bridge the gap between the traditional, strict application of this requirement – where nothing counts as acceptance except the completed action – and the more modern trend towards allowing offeree some time to complete the action. Like the First Restatement before it, Restatement (2d) of Contracts § 45 states that:

> If an offer for a unilateral contract is made, and part of the consideration requested in the offer is given or tendered by the offeree in response thereto, the offeror is bound by a contract, the duty of immediate performance of which is conditional on the full consideration being given or tendered within the time stated in the offer, or, if no time is stated therein, within a reasonable time.

This is somewhat more complicated than a simple rejection of the original conception of the unilateral contract requiring a completed action for acceptance. Under the original conception, unilateral and bilateral contracts were the same in one essential respect; each involved a straightforward quid pro quo – *you give me this, I give you that*. Of course, "*this*" was different in each case. In the bilateral contract it could be a promise, but in the unilateral contract it had to be a completed action. Under the Restatements, however, the unilateral contract is a more complex construction – *you give me this, and promise to complete this other, I give you that and promise to let you finish this other, except if you don't give me this other, then I don't have to give you that.*[4]

The idea seems to be that the offeror's implicit "subsidiary promise" precludes the unseemly (and arguably unjust) situation in which the offer is yanked out from under offeree in the midst of the latter's attempt to complete the requested action. There is some suggestion in the official comments to § 45 that this modern position is a recognition of the offeree's reasonable reliance on the offer, resulting in a foreseeable change in the offeree's position. Thus, the justification underlying the original approach - the absence of consideration until offeree completes the action – falls away once we recognize the part performance of the bargained-for exchange as consideration for the offeror's promise. Moreover, reference in the comments to § 90 goes even further, suggesting that consideration for the offeror's promise may not even be necessary to give the offeree the right to complete the action if there has been detrimental reliance on the offer.[5]

This is not to suggest that the doctrine of unilateral contract has been superseded as a

---

[2] Rest. (2d) Contracts § 30.

[3] *Id.* § 32.

[4] Rest. (2d) Contracts § 45, comment b., explains that the "main offer includes as a subsidiary promise, necessarily implied, that if part of the requested performance is given, the offeror will not revoke his offer, and that if tender is made it will be accepted. Part performance or tender may thus furnish consideration for the subsidiary promise. Moreover, merely acting in justifiable reliance on an offer may in some cases serve as sufficient reason for making a promise binding (see § 90)."

[5] *Cf., e.g., Northwestern Engineering Co. v. Ellerman*, 69 S.D. 397, 408, 10 N.W.2d 879, 884 (1943) (offerors "should have reasonably expected [their promise] would induce the plaintiff to submit a bid based thereon to the Government, that such promise did induce this action, and that injustice can be avoided only by enforcement of the promise").

significant legal category. To the contrary, modern cases recognize it as a basis for bind-ing a party in contract.[6] Furthermore, there are still jurisdictions that continue their ad-herence to the earlier doctrine of unilateral contract under certain circumstances, despite § 45.[7]

Another issue is whether the offeree must give notice to the offeror of an intention to perform the requested action. That, of course, is one of the central issues in *Carlill v. Carbolic Smoke Ball Co.*, [1893] 1 Q.B. 256. As Baron Bowen put it,

> One cannot doubt that, as an ordinary rule of law, an acceptance of an offer made ought to be notified to the person who makes the offer, in order that the two minds may come together. . . . But there is this clear gloss to be made upon that doctrine, that as notifica-tion of acceptance is required for the benefit of the person who makes the offer, the per-son who makes the offer may dispense with notice to himself, if he thinks it desirable to do so. . . . [I]f the person making the offer, expressly or impliedly intimates in his offer that it will be sufficient to act on the proposal without communicating acceptance of it to himself, performance of the condition is a sufficient acceptance without notification.

Carlill, 1 Q.B. at 269-270. In other words, one expects the offeror to be on notice about attempts to complete the requested action, but that notice may be provided by practical circumstances or by offeree's notification, or it may be dispensed with if offeror so chooses.

III. NOT SO SWEET CHARITY

Last year's fund-raising auction for the school's Public Legal Services Society (PLSS) was a disaster. As is the usual practice for this auction, faculty members were asked to donate goods and services. As usual, Professor Badlaw donated "Breakfast with me at Café Reynaldo for whomever contributes at least $100.00 to the PLSS." During the auction, Law School Dean Baaatz made the winning bid for breakfast with the professor. As Dean Baaatz was walking up to the auction table to pay, Professor Badlaw rose from his seat and said – loudly – "I withdraw the offer!" Pandemonium ensued.

The end result was that the Professor made a donation to the PLSS in an amount equal to the winning bid, but the Dean did not get a breakfast with the Professor at Café Reynaldo. Since the PLSS received the amount it would have received in any event, it did not even consider making a claim on the basis that it had solicited support based on the mutually pledged donations of all contributors.[8] There was a rumor that the Dean

---

[6] *See, e.g., Dahl v. HEM Pharmaceuticals*, 7 F.3d 1399, 1404 (9th Cir. 1993), citing *Hamer v. Sidway*, 124 N.Y. 538, 27 N.E. 256 (Ct. Appeals 1891) (finding that one who participated in an extended clinical drug trial had a unilateral contract, requiring drug company to provide one-year free supply of experimental drug).

[7] *See, e.g., White v. Hugh Chatham Memorial Hosp., Inc.*, 97 N.C.App. 130, 131-132, 387 S.E.2d 80, 81 (N.C.App. 1990) (stating that the "offeror is the master of his offer [of a unilateral contract] and can withdraw it at any time before it is accepted by performance"). *Cf. In re Pettin-gill*, 403 B.R. 624 (Bankr. E.D. Ark. 2009) (dicta).

[8] *Cf., e.g., Ricketts v. Scothorn*, 57 Neb. 51, 77 N.W. 365, 366 (1898) ("[I]t has often been held that an action on a note given to a church, college, or other like institution, upon the faith of which money has been expended or obligations incurred, could not be successfully defended on the ground of a want of consideration. . . . [T]he decision is generally put on the ground that the ex-penditure of money or assumption of liability by the donee on the faith of the promise constitutes a

wanted to sue Professor Badlaw, but deans are just that way.

Your classmate Edgar Beaver is the chair of this year's PLSS Auction Organizing Committee, and he most assuredly does not want any incidents this year. He wants you to look over the invitation that PLSS used last year to solicit donations for the Auction. He has asked you to look over this material and recommend changes in the text that might either make it clear to potential donors (like Professor Badlaw, for example) what they are committing to, or make it less likely that a donor would be able to pull out once the auction is under way.

Here is the text of the email solicitation that was used last year:

Dear Professors,

The PLSS event and auction will be held on March 15, 2014 at the Sherbet Grand Hotel. It will be a festive event, light on speechmaking and heavy on socializing with alums and students and eating great food. All money raised will go to PLSS, either to fund public interest placements for students during the summer or into the PLSS endowment, or both.

I am writing to ask you to contribute donations for the auction. There will be students at the event (they have a reduced ticket price) and they particularly enjoy bidding on items that Faculty donate. Whether it is a game, tickets to a play or concert, a meal, a stay at a cabin, or an outing with you, the students would welcome receiving it to auction off.

To donate an auction item, please fill out the attached form and send it to Antonia Coiffure, PLSS Board Member, at a_coiffure@u.pacman.edu.

If instead of donating an item, you would like to make a charitable gift, please see the link in the PLSS web page, which also tells you how to buy tickets for the auction.

It is hard to overstate the importance of these summer internships to the students. It gives them a chance to contribute to the public interest in an employment context while gaining valuable job experience. Also, every year we use the endowment fund to help defray student loan debt for graduates working in public interest jobs and earning very little money. The debt is so high, and their wages so small, that our committee always wishes we had more money to distribute. Nonetheless, what we have makes a difference for graduates, and I hope that we will continue to build it.

Thank you in advance for your donations to PLSS.

---

valuable and sufficient consideration.").

Here is the text of the donation form that was attached to last year's email solicitation:

Pacman U. Anniversary Celebration Benefiting Public Legal Services Society (PLSS)

DONOR & CONTACT INFORMATION

Name/Contact   _____ *

       Class   _____ *

Company   _____ *

Address 1   _____ *

Address 2   _____

City   _____ *

State   _____ *

Zip   _____ *

Phone   _____ *

Contact e-mail   _____ *

*Required information

Continued on reverse side

AUCTION ITEM INFORMATION

Item Description (Please give a detailed description of item or service being donated):

_____

_____

Estimated Fair Market Value $ _____

(*Per IRS regulations, we do not assign values to in-kind gifts. The donor must provide this information.*)

Status of Donation: ☐ Item Enclosed
☐ Gift Certificate Enclosed*
☐ Item to be Delivered
☐ This agreement serves as a gift certificate.*
☐ Item to be Picked Up

* Unless otherwise specified, donor agrees that certificate(s) will be valid until 3/15/15.

Cash Donation: $ _____

Payment Method: ☐ Check, payable to University of Pacman
School of Law
☐ Credit Card: ☐Visa ☐MC ☐Am Ex ☐Discover

Card number: ▨▨▨ ▨▨▨ ▨▨▨ ▨▨▨ Exp. Date __ __

Billing address _____

_____ Zip _____

Signature _____ Date _____

DONOR RECOGNITION

☐ Donor name should read: _____
☐ I/We wish to remain anonymous.

Thanks for your support! Your gift is tax-deductible as provided by law.
Federal Tax ID: 94-1234567

Before responding to Edgar's question, consider whether these documents are sufficient to create an enforceable unilateral contract. Are changes necessary for such a contract to be formed? Be very detailed and specific in your reasoning, because your client may want every change explained. Think about *why* the suggested changes would either make the terms of the unilateral contract clear to donors and bidders, or make it less likely that a donor would be able to revoke their promised donation once the auction is under way.

CHAPTER SIX

INTERPRETATION

I. INTRODUCTION

How often have you bought a product – think mass-market consumer software, for example – with a "shrinkwrap" sticker (terms contained on or inside the software box)? How about "clickwrap" terms (terms appearing on screen when the consumer clicks to install the software)? If you are like the vast majority of consumers, you probably did not spend a lot of time pondering what the terms meant, if you even read them. This simulation considers contract interpretation issues in the context of shrinkwrapped products.

II. OVERVIEW OF THE LAW

Typically, discussion about shrinkwrap and clickwrap focuses on assent and contract formation[1] – *e.g.*, unseen/unknown terms, "rolling contract formation,"[2] and the like. These situations raise a basic but vexing contracts issue: Are the contract terms within the shrink-wrap or behind the clickwrap – sometimes unavailable for review until after payment – enforceable against the purchaser? Some courts have found that the shrink-wrapped terms are indeed enforceable, holding that the purchaser has assented to the terms by installation or use of the software.[3] On the other hand, some courts have refused to enforce shrinkwrap or clickwrap agreements, holding them instead to be counter-offers, or proposals for additional terms with respect to contracts already formed.[4] As a practical matter, however, most consumers (even most *Contracts* professors) probably don't ever bother to read the terms, let alone consider the long-term implications of them as applied to their use of a product. If the price point of the product is low enough, it is unlikely that an individual consumer will seriously explore his or her possible contract

---

[1] *See, e.g., Step–Saver Data Systems, Inc. v. Wyse Technology*, 939 F.2d 91 (3d Cir. 1991) (holding that "box top" terms were material alterations to terms of a previously formed contract, not part of the contract absent express agreement of purchaser *per* UCC § 2-207(2)(b)); *ProCD, Inc. v. Zeidenberg*, 86 F.3d 1447 (7th Cir. 1996) (rejecting application of UCC §§ 2-207 and 2-209; distinguishing *Step-Saver*); *Hill v. Gateway 2000, Inc.*, 105 F.3d 1147 (7th Cir. 1997) (expanding application of *ProCD* to include not only software licensing but also hardware goods; rejecting argument that defendant seller had failed to give plaintiff buyers adequate notice of arbitration clause inside box containing purchased hardware). *See also Brower v. Gateway 2000*, 246 A.D.2d 246, 250-251, 676 N.Y.S.2d 569, 572 (App.Div.1998) (discussing *Hill* and *Pro-CD* with approval).

[2] *See* John E. Murray, Jr. & Harry M. Flechtner, *The Summer, 1999 Draft of Revised Article 2 of the Uniform Commercial Code: What Hath NCCUSL Rejected?*, 19 J.L. & COM. 1, 34 (1999) (characterizing *Pro-CD* analysis as "a 'layered' or 'rolling contract' formation analysis").

[3] *See, e.g., I.Lan Systems, Inc. v. Netscout Service Level Corp.*, 183 F. Supp. 2d 328 (D. Mass. 2002) (applying Massachusetts law to clickwrap agreement).

[4] For an excellent discussion of the competing positions in this regard, see Murray & Flechtner, *supra* note 2.

rights. Inertia takes over, and the consumer is more likely simply to replace a product that has disappointed. In broader market terms, however, if a sufficient number of consumers are disappointed, collective action might result, either in consumer movement away from the product or in class action litigation that might tee up the enforceability issue for judicial resolution.

What is rarely explored, however, are the interpretation issues that may arise in understanding and applying such contract terms. One problem that needs to be explored concerns the *context* within which the party is supposed to interpret the contract. There is rarely any bargaining or even discussion about the terms between the parties, because the terms are after the fact of the purchase. This anomaly is one of the things that makes the approach of *Step–Saver* so attractive:

> Step–Saver would typically purchase copies of the program in the following manner. First, Step–Saver would telephone [codefendant The Software Link (TSL)] and place an order. (Step–Saver would typically order twenty copies of the program at a time.) TSL would accept the order and promise, while on the telephone, to ship the goods promptly. After the telephone order, Step–Saver would send a purchase order, detailing the items to be purchased, their price, and shipping and payment terms. TSL would ship the order promptly, along with an invoice. The invoice would contain terms essentially identical with those on Step–Saver's purchase order: price, quantity, and shipping and payment terms. No reference was made during the telephone calls, or on either the purchase orders or the invoices with regard to a disclaimer of any warranties.
>
> Printed on the package of each copy of the program, however, would be a copy of the box-top license. The box-top license contains five terms relevant to this action:
>
>> (1) The box-top license provides that the customer has not purchased the software itself, but has merely obtained a personal, non-transferable license to use the program.
>>
>> (2) The box-top license, in detail and at some length, disclaims all express and implied warranties except for a warranty that the disks contained in the box are free from defects.
>>
>> (3) The box-top license provides that the sole remedy available to a purchaser of the program is to return a defective disk for replacement; the license excludes any liability for damages, direct or consequential, caused by the use of the program.
>>
>> (4) The box-top license contains an integration clause, which provides that the box-top license is the final and complete expression of the terms of the parties's agreement.
>>
>> (5) The box-top license states: "Opening this package indicates your acceptance of these terms and conditions. If you do not agree with them, you should promptly return the package unopened to the person from whom you purchased it within fifteen days from date of purchase and your money will be refunded to you by that person."

Step-Saver, 939 F.2d at 95-97 (footnote omitted). There are all sorts of interprettive issues embedded in the terms of this "box-top license." Take an obvious example – Is this a purchase of the program or merely "a personal, non-transferable license to use the program," as clause 1 insists? Are clause 1 and clause 3 inconsistent on this point? However, if *Step-Saver* is correct, we need not resolve these interpretive issues, because the box-top terms are mere suggestions for modification of an existing contract, suggestions to which the purchaser has not acceded.

Since *Pro-CD* and its progeny reject the *Step-Saver* approach, establishing a context within which to interpret terms in dispute becomes essential. *Pro-CD* does attempt to identify such a context, when it says:

> If ProCD had to recover all of its costs and make a profit by charging a single price – that is, if it could not charge more to commercial users than to the general public – it would have to raise the price substantially over $150. The ensuing reduction in sales would harm consumers who value the information at, say, $200. They get consumer surplus of $50 under the current arrangement but would cease to buy if the price rose substantially. If because of high elasticity of demand in the consumer segment of the market the only way to make a profit turned out to be a price attractive to commercial users alone, then all consumers would lose out – and so would the commercial clients, who would have to pay more for the listings because ProCD could not obtain any contribution toward costs from the consumer market.
>
> To make price discrimination work, however, the seller must be able to control arbitrage. . . . That arbitrage would break down the price discrimination and drive up the minimum price at which ProCD would sell to anyone.

ProCD, Inc. v. Zeidenberg, 86 F.3d at 1450. So part of the context against which we interpret the terms is the market structure prevalent for products with distinct commercial and consumer applications. There are other tools available to us in trying to interpret contract language. *See, e.g.*, REST. 2d § 202 (providing interpretive rules). The UCC gives us one compact set of interpretive sources in §§ 1-303 (defining *course of performance*, *course of dealing*, and *usage of trade*, and setting their parameters), 2-202 (allowing for the use of these sources to "explain[ ] or supplement[ ]" written contract terms). However, the cases recognize that the extrinsic sources that aid in interpretation are broader than those idetified in UCC § 1-303. (One excellent guide is *Frigaliment Importing Co. v. B.N.S. Intern. Sales Corp.*, 190 F.Supp. 116 (S.D.N.Y. 1960) – **yes, the chicken case** – which walks us through a variety of interpretive sources.

III. THE CASE OF THE SHRINKWRAPPED CASEBOOK

For purposes of this simulation, you are . . . you – a law student trying to make your way through the law school experience. Your classmate Edgar Beaver is considering whether to buy a new copy of the assigned contracts casebook at the Bookstore or a used copy from a 2L. Edgar is examining the casebook in the Bookstore, and he notices that it is sealed in plastic, so he obviously can't thumb through it to experience that "new book" smell. After he buys the book, he notices that there is a little sticker attached to the front of the book, with very small print.

This is the book

And here's the sticker:

Questions

A. Recognizing you as a nascent *Contracts* aficionado, Edgar has asked your advice with respect to his purchase of the casebook. After he explains to you what "nascent" means, you agree to assist him. Assume for present purposes that there *is* a contract for the sale of the book and access to online content, and that it includes the terms on the shrinkwrap sticker.[5] In answering the following questions, you must decide *what* the terms mean and *how* they apply.

     1. If Edgar buys the casebook at the Bookstore, but when he unwraps it at home he discovers that it is full of typographical errors and blank pages, does he have the right to return the casebook for a full refund?

     2. What if he buys the casebook at the Bookstore, but when he unwraps it at home, he discovers on the inside front cover a written notice from the publisher stating that, "as a condition of purchase," he agrees to "pay the publisher $3,500 if he writes and posts a negative review of the casebook, the authors," or the publisher? Would he be liable to the publisher for any negative comments about these terms that he posts on his Contracts professor's TWEN® site?

     3. Would it make any difference to either of your previous answers if, taking a closer look, Edgar actually reads the sticker *before* buying the casebook at the Bookstore, and tells the Bookstore sales clerk "I do not accept the terms on this sticker" *and then* pays for the casebook and leaves with it?

B. According to REST. 2d § 202(1), we should interpret the terms of the contract "in the light of all the circumstances," with particular attention to "the principal purpose of the parties" if it is ascertainable. So what are "all the circumstances" in this situation?[6]

C. *If* this is primarily a sale of goods, then UCC §§ 1-303 and 2-202 apply.[7] Is there any usage of trade that would be relevant to our problem? *See also* REST. 2d § 202(5). Presumably Edgar has bought other casebooks. Is there any course of dealing that might be relevant?

---

     [5] You could, of course, attack those terms as *not* being part of the contract for the sale of the book, in accordance with what you learned in the problem in Chapter 1, but that is another story.

     [6] According to REST. 2d § 202, comment b.,

> The meaning of words and other symbols commonly depends on their context; the meaning of other conduct is even more dependent on the circumstances. In interpreting the words and conduct of the parties to a contract, a court seeks to put itself in the position they occupied at the time the contract was made. When the parties have adopted a writing as a final expression of their agreement, interpretation is directed to the meaning of that writing in the light of the circumstances. See §§ 209, 212. *The circumstances for this purpose include the entire situation, as it appeared to the parties, and in appropriate cases may include facts known to one party of which the other had reason to know.* See § 201.

(Emphasis added.)

     [7] That would not preclude use of the interpretive rules in REST. 2d § 202, however. According to REST. 2d § 202, comment a., "The rules in this Section are applicable to all manifestations of intention and all transactions. The rules are general in character, and serve merely as guides in the process of interpretation."

D. Is there anything in the terms of the contract as we know it that would exclude a cause of action for breach of warranty? *Cf.* UCC §§ 2-315 - 2-316 (requirements for exclusion or modification of implied warranty of fitness for particular use). (Note that § 2-316 itself refers us to the interpretive rules of § 2-202 in resolving this issue.)

E. What guidance would a case like *Frigaliment* offer us in trying to interpret the meaning and application of the terms of the contract? We should consider in succession the following interpretive sources:

1. *The language of the contract itself.* "Since the word ['non-returnable'] standing alone is ambiguous, I turn first to see whether the contract itself offers any aid to its interpretation." *Frigaliment Importing Co.*, 190 F.Supp. at 118. Is it relevant that the "non-returnability" language appears on the sticker announcing the online access? Could we argue that the "non-returnabilty" of the book is really a concern about the retention of software access in the absence of the book purchase, so that reasonable complaints about the fitness of the book itself should still allow for return of the book?

2. *Trade usage and other examples of extrinsic practice.* Is it possible that there is "a definite trade usage that ['book'] meant ['a usable book']"? *Id.* at 119. We need to know more about common practices in the law book trade. For example, is there a non-returnable policy for books that do *not* bundle software with the book purchase? *See also id.* at 120-121 (discussing the relevance of party conduct to interpretation of contract tersm).

3. *Regulatory context.* Is it possible that "the contract incorporated [government] regulations by reference" that might help explain the meaning and effect of the sticker language? *Id.* at 120. As a practical matter, that is not very likely in our particular case, but in our highly regulated society, this is probably worth keeping in mind as a possibility. For example, *Step-Saver* suggested that some of the box-top terms were actually focused on copyright law implications, not contract at all,[8] and such extrinsic concerns might influence the way we interpreted the terms for contract law purposes.

4. *Structure and pricing of the market.* Whether and what the parties "must likewise have known [about] the market" could influence the way we interpret the terms. *Frigaliment Importing Co.*, 190 F.Supp. at 120. This is, of course, a decisive consideration in *Pro-CD*. Is the pirating of online content a concern in the law book market? In the absence of broad restrictions on returns, would the publisher be forced to raise prices to cover risks of piracy?

---

[8] *See Step-Saver*, 939 F.2d at 95 n.7:

When these form licenses were first developed for software, it was, in large part, to avoid the federal copyright law first sale doctrine. Under the first sale doctrine, once the copyright holder has sold a copy of the copyrighted work, the owner of the copy could "sell or otherwise dispose of the possession of that copy" without the copyright holder's consent. *See Bobbs–Merrill Co. v. Straus*, 210 U.S. 339, 350, 28 S.Ct. 722, 726, 52 L.Ed. 1086 (1908); 17 U.S.C.A. § 109(a) (West 1977).

CHAPTER SEVEN

THE PAROL EVIDENCE RULE

I. INTRODUCTION

The Parol Evidence Rule is a rule of contract interpretation. Don't let its name confuse you. It is not about whether evidence is admissible in court. It is a rule designed to help you identify the terms of a contract. Another source of confusion is that the word "parol" may suggest that it only applies to spoken words. Actually, the rule helps us understand the significance of spoken and written communications, and whether they are part of a final agreement. The Parol Evidence Rule can be used to clarify unclear agreements when the parties had a series of written communications or when the parties discussed an agreement and then signed written terms that might not match their actual understanding.

II. OVERVIEW OF THE LAW

The rule provides that "a final agreement supersedes tentative terms discussed in earlier negotiations."[1] It bars courts from considering prior discussions or written drafts once the final agreement has been made. It assumes that an older inconsistent term was discarded in favor of the term that was used in the final agreement. Here is an example of how it works.

Before two people make an agreement, they negotiate. Consider the following negotiation. When an executive applies for a job, he asks for $250,000, six weeks of paid vacation every year and benefits. The company responds that most start vice president positions at $175,00 with two weeks vacation. The executive explains that he always take his wife to Manhattan to see plays for three weeks and does not want the job without at least four weeks vacation. He explains he also does not want to give up his annual trip to Las Vegas with his college buddies. Thinking about a woman who took time off to care for a terminally ill parent, the President said that occasionally, extraordinary circumstances justify additional time off, but it is not our normal practice. Ultimately, the company offers the executive a final deal (and written contract) of $175,000 in salary and three weeks vacation. The executive believes that he will become a rising star in the organization and will earn additional time off so he signs the deal.

When it comes time for that trip to Las Vegas, he may want to take a fourth week off. Then, the parties will turn to the contract to look at how much vacation they agreed on. The Parol Evidence Rule helps the parties (and a court) sort out whether subjective expectations, prior discussions or the written contract spell out the terms of the deal. The Parol Evidence Rule provides that generally, the terms of the contract are the best meas-

---

[1] JOSEPH M. PERILLO, CONTRACTS § 3.2 at 113 (7th ed. 2014).

ure of the parties' objective understanding.[2] Based on this rule, the prior conversations and the employee's subjective expectation of more vacation are not part of the agreement. Instead, in this situation, the rule makes it easy. It instructs us to ignore the prior discussions and the employee's expectation and look at the actual number of vacation weeks negotiated and written into the contract. Generally, the Parol Evidence Rule blocks consideration of prior negotiations if the meaning of a term in a final agreement is clear.[3]

The media mogul Howard Stern ran into this rule when his Satellite radio network Sirius merged with XM radio. The agreement between his production company and Sirius provided that Stern would get millions in additional compensation if customer numbers exceed expectations by over 2,000,000 subscribers.[4] When Sirius and XM merged, Stern's understanding of the parties' deal was that he should be compensated for the new accounts.[5] Because the term "Sirius" was clearly defined, and the agreement provided for separate compensation in the event of an XM merger, the court ruled that there was no question of fact to be decided by a jury and granted Sirius XM Radio's motion for summary judgment.[6] The court declined to consider extrinsic evidence because the plain language of the contract made it clear that the new listeners should not be counted as "Sirius" subscribers.[7]

Sometimes the terms of the written document are not clear, and additional evidence may be necessary to understand the actual agreement. For these situations, the Parol Evidence Rule has exceptions. At common law, if the meaning of a term is ambiguous, evidence that clarifies the parties' actual agreement may be admitted.[8] That evidence may come in different forms such as the general understanding of a term in a particular industry or testimony about the parties' actions showing they proceeded under a common understanding.[9] Under the UCC, trade usage and course of performance may always be considered to understand the terms of an agreement.[10]

The Parol Evidence Rule gives courts a standard to determine when they can look at evidence outside the written document to identify the terms of the agreement. The general rule is that they cannot do so. It is designed to help courts determine what the actual agreement is between the parties. Sometimes, the actual agreement is reflected in a document signed by the parties. In other situations, the parties may sign a form that does not truly reflect their agreement. The rule gives courts guidance on whether to admit additional evidence to in order to find the meaning of the agreement between the parties.

III. CRIMSON TIDINGS TO ALL

Examine this following scenario to determine how the Parol Evidence Rule helps resolve the dispute between an artist and the University of Alabama.

---

[2] *Id.* § 3.2.

[3] E. ALAN FARNSWORTH, CONTRACTS 415 (4th ed. 2004); Unif.Commercial Code (UCC) § 2-202. Final Written Expression: Parol or Extrinsic Evidence.

[4] *One Twelve, Inc. v. Sirius XM Radio Inc.*, 2012 WL 10007771 (N.Y.Sup. Ct.).

[5] *Id.* at *4.

[6] *Id.* at *5.

[7] *Id.*

[8] Rest. (2d) Contracts §§ 209, 213 (1981).

[9] 12 Williston on Contracts § 34:7 (4th ed. 1993).

[10] UCC § 2-202(a).

Daniel Moore is a painter who loves to capture the action and community spirit of college sports on canvas. Daniel begins his artistic process by photographing multiple images of his subjects. From these photos, he studies the anatomy of the action and then creates elaborate pencil drawings. After he is satisfied with a composition, he sketches out the drawing on a large scale, and begins to paint. A single painting often takes more than six months to complete and sells for thousands of dollars. To make his art accessible to those with more modest means, Moore sells reproductions of his original art as prints and on t-shirts, posters and calendars.

Here is a reproductiion of one of the preparatory pencil drawings:

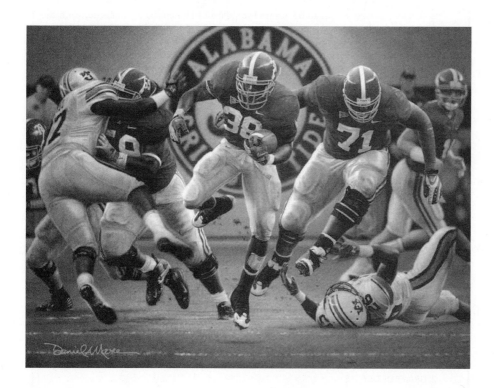

Daniel, his wife and daughters all attended the University of Alabama. The Crimson Tide's famous players and historic moments from their games are Daniel's favorite subjects. For more than twenty years, Moore's paintings have been on display in a University of Alabama gallery. The Alabama students and alumni adore Moore's work because his paintings and prints celebrate great moments in their sports history.

The University approached Moore to say that it would like to sell three of his prints in frames that are embellished with the University logo. Alabama asked Moore to create three framed prints, each to be sold for under $100 in packaging indicating that they are officially licensed by the University. The University asked Moore to sign the following contract:

The Collegiate Licensing Company License Agreement
to Use Licensed Indicia of Member Universities

This is an Agreement between _____New Life Art_____ a CORPORATION or-ganized under the laws of the state of ALABAMA having its principal place of business at _____3600 Lornaridge Dr. Birmingham, AL 35216_____ ("Licensee"), and The Col-legiate Licensing Company, a Georgia corporation, having its principal place of business at 320 Interstate North, Suite 102, Atlanta, Georgia 30339 ("CLC").

WHEREAS CLC represents licensing interests of various colleges and universities, and has the exclusive rights, as agent, to license for commercial purposes the use of certain indicia.

WHEREAS Licensee desires to be licensed to utilize certain indicia in connection with the manufacture, distribution and sale of certain products, and CLC is willing, subject to certain con-ditions, to grant such a license.

NOW, THEREOFRE, in consideration of the parties' mutual covenants and undertakings and other good and valuable consideration the receipt and sufficiency of such are acknowledged, the parties agree as follows:

1. DEFINITIONS

(a) "Member Universities" means the colleges and universities currently represented by CLC including any additions or deletions as from time to time may be made by CLC.

(b) "Licensed Indicia" means the names, symbols, designs, and colors of the Member Uni-versities, including without limitation, the trademarks, service marks, designs, team names, nicknames, abbreviations, city/state names in the appropriate context, slogans, logographics, mascots, seals and other symbols associated with or referring to the respective Member univer-sities. Licensed Indicia includes those in Appendix B and indicia adopted, used and approved for use by the Member Universities. Any newly adopted indicia shall be deemed to be additions to the Licensed Indicia in Appendix B and shall be subject to the terms and conditions of the Agreement.

(c) "Licensed Articles" means the products listed in Appendix C and bearing Licensed Indi-cia.
\/\

\/\

2. GRANT OF LICENSE

(a) Grant: CLC grants to Licensee the nonexclusive, nontransferable license to use the Li-censed Indicia on the Licensed Articles for Retail Sales in the Territory during the Term. This li-cense applies only to the Member Universities listed on Appendix A and any changes thereto; the approved use of the Licensed Indicia shown on Appendix B and any changes thereto; and, the approved Licensed Articles described in Appendix C and any changes thereto.

(b) Territory: The Territory is the United States of America, its territories and possessions, the Commonwealth of Puerto Rico, and United States military bases abroad. Licensee shall not distribute or sell Licensed Articles outside the Territory, or to any person or entity that Licensee knows or has reason to know intends or is likely to resell Licensed Articles outside the Territory.

(c) Term: This Agreement shall begin effect on the last date of signature below and shall expire 6/30/96 unless terminated sooner or extended in the manner provided in this Agree-ment.
\/\

VVV

(f) Limitation of License: This license is subject to the following additional limitations.

(1) Licensee shall not use the Licensed indicia for any purpose other than upon or in connection with the approved Licensed Articles listed in Appendix C. Any additions to the Licensed Articles and/or new designs shall be submitted in writing to CLC and samples shall be submitted to CLC for prior written approval. Licensee shall, upon request by CLC immediately recall any unauthorized products or designs from the marketplace, and destroy or submit to CLC at licensee's expense said products or designs, at CLC's option.

(2) Licensee shall not provide any method of application of Licensed Indicia to any party unless CLC authorizes Licensee to provide said application under the terms of an authorized manufacturer's agreement.

(3) Licensee shall not contract with any party for the production or application of Licensed indicia by that party ("Manufacturer") without CLC's authorization. In the event that Licensee desires to have a Manufacturer produce one or more Licensed Article, or any component thereof, Licensee shall provide CLC with the name, address, telephone number and name of the principal contact of the proposed Manufacturer. CLC must approve any Manufacturer, and the Manufacturer must execute an authorized manufacturer's or supplier's agreement provided by CLC prior to use of the Licensed Indicia. In addition, Licensee shall take the steps necessary to ensure the following: Manufacturer produces the Licensed Articles only as and when directed by the Licensee, which remains fully responsible for ensuring that the Licensed Articles are manufactured in accordance with the terms herein including approval; Manufacturer does not distribute, sell or supply the Licensed Articles to any person or entity other than Licensee. Manufacturer does not delegate in any manner whatsoever its obligations with respect to the Licensed Articles. Licensee's failure to comply with this Paragraph may result in termination of this Agreement and/or confiscation and seizure of licensed Articles. CLC hereby reserves the right to terminate in its discretion the engagement of any Manufacturer at any time.

(4) Licensee shall not engage in the direct shipment of off-shore manufactured Licensed Articles to distributors, wholesalers, retailers, etc. Licensee must take receipt of Licensed Articles at the applicable U.S. port of entry.

(5) Licensee shall not manufacture, sell, or distribute articles bearing Licensed Indicia as Premiums, for publicity purposes, for fund raising, as giveaways, in combination sales, or for disposal under similar methods of merchandising. Licensee shall not use any of the Licensed Indicia in connection with any sweepstake, lottery, game of chance or any similar promotional or sales program. In the event Licensee desires to use Licensed Articles for acceptable promotional purposes. Licensee shall obtain written approval from CLC.

(6) Licensee is not permitted, without the applicable Member University's prior consent, to promote or market a Licensed Article by means of a direct mailing or any other direct solicitation to a list of alumni, students, parents, athletic contributors, faculty or staff, or other group associated with the Member University, regardless of how Licensee acquires such list.

VVVVVVVVVVVVVVVVVVVVVVVVVVVVVVVVVVVVVVVVVVVVVVVVVVVV

VVVVVVVVVVVVVVVVVVVVVVVVVVVVVVVVVVVVVVVVVVVVVVVVVVVV

5. NONEXCLUSIVITY

Nothing in this Agreement shall be construed to prevent CLC or any Member University from granting any other licenses for use of the Licensed Indicia.

VVVVVVVVVVVVVVVVVVVVVVVVVVVVVVVVVVVVVVVVVVVVVVVVVVVV

∿∿

11. OWNERSHIP OF LICENSED INDICIA AND PROTECTION OF RIGHTS

(c) Licensee recognizes the great value of the good will associated with the Licensed Indicia and acknowledges that such good will belongs to the Member Universities, and that such Licensed Indicia have secondary meaning. Licensee shall not, during the term of this Agreement or thereafter, attack the property rights of the Member Universities, attack the ___ of this Agreement, or use the Licensed Indicia or any similar mark in any manner other than as licensed hereunder.

(e) Nothing in this Agreement gives Licensee any right, title, or interest in any Licensed Indicia except the right to use in accordance with the terms of this Agreement. Licensee's use of any Licensed Indicia inures to the benefit of the respective Member University.

(g) Licensee acknowledges that its breach or threatened breach of this Agreement will result in immediate and irremediable damage to CLC and/or the Member Universities and that money damages alone would be inadequate to compensate CLC and/or the Member Universities. Therefore, in the event of a breach or threatened breach of this Agreement, by Licensee, CLC and/or the Member Universities may, in addition to other remedies, immediately obtain and enforce injunctive relief prohibiting the breach or threatened breach or compelling specific performance. In the event of any breach or threatened breach of this Agreement by Licensee or infringement of any rights of the Member Universities, if CLC employs attorneys or incurs other expenses. Licensee shall reimburse CLC for its reasonable attorney's fees and other expenses.

∿∿

∿∿

27. NO WAIVER, MODIFICATION, ETC.

This agreement, including appendices, constitutes the entire agreement and understanding between the parties and cancels, terminates, and supersedes any prior agreement or understanding relating to the subject matter hereof.

IN WITNESS WHEREOF, the parties hereto have signed this agreement

LICENSEE   <u>New Life Art</u>

by: _____
(Signature of officer, partner, or individual authorized to sign)

Title: _____

Date: _____

THE COLLEGIATE LICENSING COMPANY

by: _____
(Signature of officer, partner, or individual authorized to sign)

Title: _____

Date: _____

Questions

A. The University of Alabama has hired you to review the contract. Do you recommend that they make any changes before sending it to Moore? Before crafting your answer, what are your general impressions of the contract? Is it clear? Will it be easy for the parties to use to structure their relationship? Does the contract look like it was written especially for these parties or does it appear to be a form agreement?

B. Moore already had a conversation with the Alabama licensing agent in which Moore agreed to sell three of his prints in the store. Now that you know about this conversation, what is the legal significance of sending the written agreement to Moore? Is it important to know more about the conversation between Moore and the agent? Or does the written agreement provide all the information you need to determine the terms of the contract? The Alabama Statute of Frauds provides:

Alabama Code - Section 7-2-201: FORMAL REQUIREMENTS; STATUTE OF FRAUDS

(1) Except as otherwise provided in this section a contract for the sale of goods for the price of $500 or more is not enforceable by way of action or defense unless there is some writing sufficient to indicate that a contract for sale has been made between the parties and signed by the party against whom enforcement is sought or by his authorized agent or broker. A writing is not insufficient because it omits or incorrectly states a term agreed upon, but the contract is not enforceable under this paragraph beyond the quantity of goods shown in such writing.

(2) Between merchants if within a reasonable time a writing in confirmation of the contract and sufficient against the sender is received and the party receiving it has reason to know its contents, it satisfies the requirements of subsection (1) against such party unless written notice of objection to its contents is given within 10 days after it is received.

(3) A contract which does not satisfy the requirements of subsection (1) but which is valid in other respects is enforceable:
(a) If the goods are to be specially manufactured for the buyer and are not suitable for sale to others in the ordinary course of the seller's business and the seller, before notice of repudiation is received and under circumstances which reasonably indicate that the goods are for the buyer, has made either a substantial beginning of their manufacture or commitments for their procurement; or
(b) If the party against whom enforcement is sought admits in his pleading, testimony or otherwise in court that a contract for sale was made, but the contract is not enforceable under this provision beyond the quantity of goods admitted; or
(c) With respect to goods for which payment has been made and accepted or which have been received and accepted

C. You represent Daniel Moore. The University has just sent him a copy of the contract and it would like him to sign it. Moore asks you, "Is that ok?" To answer his question, think about whether this agreement is a form. When practicable, form contracts can and often should be changed so that the written document reflects the actual agreement between the parties. Is this a contract of adhesion (a form that Daniel must agree to as it is) or does Daniel have the opportunity to change certain terms? Before advising your client, think about the purpose of the form. Why do you think it was created? Is the agreement clear? If you don't understand it, how will the parties who may have no legal training be able to understand what they are supposed to do in order to honor their agreement? Would you recommend changing any terms so that the written agreement reflects the understanding between Moore and the University?

D. Assume that Moore signed the contract without reading it and without seeking legal advice. The University then asks Moore to stop creating any works that depict the Alabama uniforms and their distinctive crimson and white colors. Moore has asked you to explain whether he gave up those rights by signing this agreement.

This question presents you with a situation in which some sort of agreement was formed. For review purposes, you may begin by identifying the offer and acceptance, and whether the agreement is supported by consideration. Once you have done that analysis, it is important to ask whether other contract doctrines might help your client. Daniel Moore believes he has the right to paint Alabama football scenes without the University's permission. For now, please set aside the interesting intellectual property and First Amendment issues raised by his question, and assume that he once had that right. Then, think about whether Moore gave up that right by signing this contract. Did Daniel Moore expressly give up the right to paint scenes from Alabama football games? Does the contract restrict the subjects of his paintings in any way? If so, what does the contract say he agreed not to do? Does that statement reflect the actual agreement between the parties? Is there any doctrine in contract law that might help him?

E. Considering the Parol Evidence Rule, what questions do you need to ask to determine whether the rule would be used to bar evidence of other agreements or the parties' actions? One place to start is to consider whether any terms in the agreement are ambiguous or inconsistent with the actual agreement between Moore and the University. Daniel Moore claims that for more than twenty years, the University encouraged him to paint the Alabama team in their uniforms. During the term of this agreement and afterwards, he painted many scenes featuring the team in uniform in addition to the three prints he created. He believes he never agreed to give up this right. The University of Alabama reads the agreement differently, saying he did give up the right to paint the school uniforms. Assume that the parties signed the agreement but the University did not seek to enforce its rights for five years. Does it matter whether Moore continued to sell other Alabama football images during those years? Do these facts help you determine whether the contract contains an ambiguity?

CHAPTER EIGHT

MISTAKE

I. INTRODUCTION

A "mistake" is defined by the Restatement (2d) as "a belief that is not in accord with the facts."[1] Everyone makes mistakes. Sometimes a mistake may just be embarrassing, like when you fumble the lyrics halfway through *Bohemian Rhapsody* while singing in the shower. You just have to carry on, as if nothing really matters. But sometimes the mistake may be more costly, like when you assume that something is covered by a contract that you have just signed, but it isn't.

In that latter context, a number of issues must be sorted out. There are mistakes that we might characterize as mistakes about externalities; *e.g.*, you thought you would enjoy learning to ski, but you forgot how much you hated the cold. There are other mistakes that we might call mistakes of behavior, as when someone assumes it doesn't matter whether one reads a contract before signing it. Finally, there are mistakes that we might consider to be content mistakes; *i.e.*, where we make a computational error or misapprehend the meaning, intention, or effect of the contract and its language.

This chapter examines whether, and to what extent, mistakes affect the formation, performance and enforcement of contracts. If we consider a particular type of mistake is pertinent to one of these contract issues, what implications flow from this situation? Does it render the contract void or voidable? Invalid? Or does a pertinent mistake affect the contract in some other way?

II. OVERVIEW OF THE LAW

The law of contracts is most likely to be sympathetic – if it is sympathetic at all – to mistakes about the circumstances or terms of a contract. Here we are talking about facts and circumstances surrounding the transaction or concerning the meaning and implications of its language that were unknown to one or both parties at the time the contract was formed. If the mistake is made by only one of the parties to the contract, it is referred to as a *unilateral mistake*. If it is made by both parties to the contract, it is referred to as a *mutual mistake*. These are typically content mistakes.

Mistakes about externalities are usually not considered redressable by contract law. These typically involve the subjective risks of satisfaction outside the specific bargain between the parties. If the parties focus on such a risk, they may of course address it in terms of, for example, a satisfaction clause, like the one in *Wood v. Duff–Gordon*,[2] but such a clause will be read as implying an obligation that the clause be exercised in good faith. An alternative approach to this problem would be to include a right to cancel within

---

[1] REST. (2d) Contracts § 151.
[2] 222 N.Y. 88, 118 N.E. 214 (1917).

a specified period after signing – a "cooling off" period intended to address problems like "buyer's remorse." Notice that these approaches involve assimilating the risk of a mistake about externalities into the contract itself and transforming it into an objective contract term.

Behavioral mistakes tend to be addressed by the law of contracts through established rules about the bargaining process itself. In various ways, these rules express a conceptual bias against behavioral mistakes as a basis for avoidance of contract obligations.[3]

Hence, when contract law refers to "mistake" as a concern, it is almost invariably addressing content mistakes of one or both parties. Traditionally, the law has made a basic distinction between unilateral and mutual mistakes.

A. Unilateral Mistake

Normally, we expect each party in contract negotiations to bear their own risks as to the formation of the contract. When does the mistake of *one* party to a contract affect the formation or enforceability of the contract? The Restatement provides guidance as to the boundaries within which relief from a unilateral mistake will be available. First, unless the mistake involves "a basic assumption on which he made the contract,"[4] a party bears the risk of his or her own mistakes. Second, the mistake must have "a material effect on the agreed exchange of performances that is adverse to him."[5] Third, relief from the mistake is not available if "the risk of the mistake" is allocated to the mistaken party.[6]

The risk of the mistake may be allocated to that party in any one of three ways. First, and most obviously, it may be that the *parties* have allocated the risk to that party in the agreement itself.[7] Assume, for example, that, when I was selling my car for $1,200.00,[8] the contract for the sale of the car included the following provision:

> The parties agree that the vehicle is sold in an "as is" condition and has not been subject to any required smog-testing in the past twelve months.

Buyer's mistaken belief that the vehicle will pass a smog test when next required by the Division of Motor Vehicles would probably not be a basis for relief under the contract of sale.[9]

Second, the risk of the mistake will be allocated to a mistaken party if he or she is "aware, at the time the contract is made, that [he or she] has only limited knowledge with

---

[3] *See, e.g.*, Cal.Pub.Con.Code § 5101(d) (allowing, under specified circumstances, relief from mistaken construction contract bid where mistake "was made in filling out the bid and not due to error in judgment or to carelessness in inspecting the site of the work, or in reading the plans or specifications").

[4] REST. (2d) Contracts § 153.

[5] *Id.* An example of a "material effect" is offered by *Elsinore Union Elementary School District v. Kastorff*, 353 P.2d 713 (Cal. 1960), in which a bidder on a construction sub-contract made a significant computational error (approximately $11,000, 7-10% of the cost of the project) in setting the price for the work. *But cf.* Cal.Pub.Con.Code § 5101 (limiting future applicability of *Elsinore Union* in specified circumstances). For a result contrary to *Elsinore Union* in a case involving approximately a $50,000 mistake in a subcontractor's bid, see *Heifetz Metal Crafts, Inc. v. Peter Kiewit Sons' Co.*, 264 F.2d 435 (8th Cir.1959).

[6] REST. (2d) Contracts § 153.

[7] REST. (2d) Contracts § 154(a).

[8] *See supra* at 3.

[9] *Cf. Lenawee County Bd. of Health v. Messerly*, 331 N.W.2d 203 (1982) (allocating risk of mistake to buyer of apartment building purchased in "as is" condition).

respect to the facts to which the mistake relates but treats [his or her] limited knowledge as sufficient."[10]

Third, the risk may be allocated to the mistaken party by a court "on the ground that it is reasonable in the circumstances to do so."[11]

In addition to deciding whether a unilateral mistake is within the boundaries where relief might be allowed, and whether the risk of the mistake has been allocated by the parties or as a matter of legal matter, contract law imposes two additional, alternative requirements that must be met before relief from the mistake will be permitted. Relief from a unilateral, unallocated risk of mistake is permitted where "the effect of the mistake is such that enforcement of the contract would be unconscionable."[12] Alternatively, relief is permitted where "the *other* party had reason to know of the mistake or [his or her] fault caused the mistake."[13]

B. Mutual Mistake

Should it make a difference to the analysis if *both* parties make a mistake concerning the same basic assumption? One peerless example of this sort of situation is offered by *Raffles v. Wichelhaus*,[14] in which the two parties to a sales contract had an entirely different ship in mind for delivery (and hence the timing of the delivery) of cotton in a price-volatile market. Apparently, the mutual mistake in that case was so material that there was no contract formed.

Of course, it is possible that a mutual mistake might not prevent contract formation, and then we need to ask what other effects might the mistake have on the contract. If the mistake simply involves a lack of awareness of the difficulty of the task under contract, arguably we have a mistake about externalities, and courts seem unsympathetic to parties seeking relief on that basis.[15] On the other hand, a mutual mistake about the subject of the contract or the quality of object being sold under the contract might be viewed as a content mistake, which may be susceptible to relief such as rescission or other damage reme-

---

[10] REST. (2d) Contracts § 154(b). *See, e.g., Estate of Nelson v. Rice*, 12 P.3d 238 (Ariz. App. 2000) (holding that seller of paintings failed to inform itself of the value of the art, and thus was allocated the risk that it had mistaken valuable paintings as worthless).

[11] REST. (2d) Contracts § 154(c). *See, e.g. Estate of Nelson, supra* (mistake due to failure of estate adequately to investigate value of paintings that it sold). *But cf. Wood v. Boynton*, 25 N.W. 42 (Wis. 1885) (jeweler failed to recognize stone as valuable uncut diamond before purchasing it from owner, but still prevails against seller's action for return of diamond); *Sherwood v. Walker*, 33 N.W. 919 (Mich. 1887) (cattle breeder failed to detect pregnancy of famous cow before agreeing to sell her as sterile, but still prevails against buyer's suit to enforce contract by replevin). *See generally Lenawee County Bd. of Health, supra* (repudiating approach adopted in court's decision in *Sherwood*; endorsing Restatement approach).

[12] REST. (2d) Contracts § 153(a). *Cf. Elsinore Union*, 353 P. 2d at 719 ("Under the circumstances the 'bargain' for which the board presses . . . appears [too] sharp for law and equity to sustain."); *Estate of Nelson, supra* (finding nothing unconscionable about terms of contract for sale of paintings mistakenly thought to be of little value).

[13] REST. (2d) Contracts § 153(b) (emphasis added).

[14] 2 H. & C. 906, 159 Eng. Rep. 375 (Exchequer 1864). For useful background and analysis of this famous case, see DOUGLAS G. BAIRD, RECONSTRUCTING CONTRACTS 9-13 (2013). *See also* A.W.B. Simpson, *Contracts for Cotton to Arrive: The Case of the Two Ships Peerless*, 11 CARDOZO L. REV. 287 (1989).

[15] *See, e.g., Dermott v. Jones*, 69 U.S. (2 Wall.) 1, 8 (1864) ("If unexpected impediments lie in the way, and a loss ensue, [contracts principle] leaves the loss where the contract places it"); *Stees v. Leonard*, 20 Minn. 494 (1874) (quoting *Dermott* with approval).

dies.[16]

In general, a mutual mistake *"at the time a contract was made* as to a basic assumption on which the contract was made has a material effect on the agreed exchange of performances" and renders the contract voidable by the party who turns out to be adversely affected by the mistake.[17] However, this rule does not apply if the party "bears the risk of the mistake"[18] as we discussed earlier in the context of unilateral mistakes.[19] On the other hand, the fact that one party was at fault in failing to know or discover the facts before making the contract does not bar him or her from a remedy of avoidance or reformation or the contract, "unless his fault amounts to a failure to act in good faith and in accordance with reasonable standards of fair dealing."[20]

The next section examines a situation in which a contract is formed by *clickwrap*.[21] Our problem is to consider whether possible mistakes about the terms of the contract and the expected performance of the parties may render the contract voidable.

III. SYSTEM ERROR

Melvin C. Witless is a management consultant who is trying to stay competitive and tech-savvy. He believes that by using the latest available technical innovations for data analysis and evaluation, he can offer his clients highly sophisticated research and recommendations and thus continue to enjoy a competitive edge in the consultancy market. Last week his 17 year old son Max told Melvin that he should replace the current operating system in his laptop with the cutting edge operating system developed by Gurgle Corp., Gurgle Brass. Melvin was a little skeptical at first, because he ran all of his analytical software on that laptop, and he needed an operating system that was compatible. Eventually, however, he decided to follow Max's advice.

Melvin went online to the Gurgle website and clicked on the button to purchase the Gurgle Brass operating system. Nothing that he read on the website suggested that there were any restrictions on the use of his software with the new operating system. He assumed that it would work fine, but he decided to take a look at the contract for the pur-

---

[16] *See, e.g., Renner v. Kehl*, 722 P.2d 262, 265 (Ariz. 1986) (involving mutual mistake concerning the adequacy of water supply under land subject of sale; holding that "The belief of the parties that adequate water supplies existed beneath the property was 'a basic assumption on which both parties made the contract,' . . . and their mutual mistake 'ha[d] such a material effect on the agreed exchange of performances as to upset the very bases of the contract.' . . . The contract was therefore voidable and the respondents were entitled to rescission."). In reaching this conclusion, *Renner* relied upon official comments to Restatement (2d) of Contracts § 152, discussed *infra*.

[17] REST. (2d) of Contracts § 152(1) (emphasis added). As to the determination of whether or not the mistake has a "material effect," the Restatement directs us to take account of "any relief by way of reformation, restitution, or otherwise." *Id*, § 152(2). What this cryptic direction means is something along the following lines. The normal remedy one might expect in a mistake situation is the voiding or rescission of the contract. *See, e.g., Renner*, 722 P.2d at 264-267 (discussing rescission and damages in mutual mistake case). However, the court should first see if any other relief may be available to either party, such as reformation of the contract consistent with the rules stated in Restatement §§ 155-156, or restitution consistent with Restatement § 158. Either remedy would lead to the preferable result of approximating the parties' expectations without destroying the contract. *See generally* REST. (2d) of Contracts § 152 cmt. d.

[18] REST. (2d) of Contracts § 152(1).

[19] *See supra*, text and accompanying notes 12-13.

[20] REST. (2d) of Contracts § 157.

[21] *See* Chapter 6, *supra*, at 35-37 (discussing clickwrap contract terms).

chase of the operating system. He didn't find a contract anywhere on the site, but he did find the following at the bottom of the page confirming his purchase:

> Your purchase of **Gurgle Brass** is subject to our Software License. To read the license terms click http://brass.gurgle.com/en-us/brass1/read-the-gurgle-software-license-terms.

Melvin clicked. And then he scrolled –

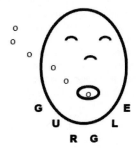

GURGLE BRASS SOFTWARE LICENSE TERMS
GURGLE BRASS PROFESSIONAL SERVICE PACK 1

These license terms are an agreement between Gurgle Corporation (or based on where you live, one of its affiliates) and you. Please read them. They apply to the software named above, which includes the media on which you received it, if any.

By using the software, you accept these terms. If you do not accept them, do not use the software. Instead, return it to the retailer for a refund or credit.

If you comply with these license terms, you have the rights below for each license you acquire.

1.   **OVERVIEW.**

a.   **Software.** The software includes desktop operating system software. This software does not include data analysis or spreadsheet services. Data analysis and spreadsheet services are available from Gurgle under a separate agreement.

b.   **License Model.** The software is licensed on a per copy per computer basis. A computer is a physical hardware system with an internal storage device capable of running the software. A hardware partition or blade is considered to be a separate computer.

2.   **INSTALLATION AND USE RIGHTS.**

a.   **One Copy per Computer.** You may install one copy of the software on one computer. That computer is the "licensed computer."

b.   **Licensed Computer.** You may use the software on up to two processors on the licensed computer at one time. Unless otherwise provided in these license terms, you may not use the software on any other computer.

c.   **Number of Users.** Unless otherwise provided in these license terms, only one user may use the software at a time.

d.   **Alternative Versions.** The software may include more than one version, such as 32-bit and 64-bit. You may install and use only one version at one time.

3.   **ADDITIONAL LICENSING REQUIREMENTS AND/OR USE RIGHTS.**

a.   **Multiplexing.** Hardware or software you use to

·   pool connections, or

·   reduce the number of devices or users that directly access or use the software (sometimes referred to as "multiplexing" or "pooling"), does not reduce the number of licenses you need.

And he scrolled –

> **b.** **Font Components.** While the software is running, you may use its fonts to display and print content. You may only
> · embed fonts in content as permitted by the embedding restrictions in the fonts; and
> · temporarily download them to a printer or other output device to print content.
>
> **c.** **Icons, images and sounds.** While the software is running, you may use but not share its icons, images, sounds, and media. The sample images, sounds and media provided with the software are for your non-commercial use only.
>
> **d.** **Use with Virtualization Technologies.** Instead of using the software directly on the licensed computer, you may install and use the software within only one virtual (or otherwise emulated) hardware system on the licensed computer. When used in a virtualized environment, content protected by digital rights management technology, BitLocker or any full volume disk drive encryption technology may not be as secure as protected content not in a virtualized environment. You should comply with all domestic and international laws that apply to such protected content.
>
> **e.** **Storage.** You may store one copy of the software on a storage device, such as a network server. You may use that copy to install the software on any other computer to which a license has been assigned.
>
> **f.** **Device Connections.** You may allow up to 20 other devices to access software installed on the licensed computer to use only File Services, Print Services, Internet Information Services and Internet Connection Sharing and Telephony Services.
>
> **g.** **Remote Access Technologies.** You may access and use the software installed on the licensed computer remotely from another device using remote access technologies as follows.
> · Remote Desktop. The single primary user of the licensed computer may access a session from any other device using Remote Desktop or similar technologies. A "session" means the experience of interacting with the software, directly or indirectly, through any combination of input, output and display peripherals. Other users may access a session from any device using these technologies, if the remote device is separately licensed to run the software.
> · Other Access Technologies. You may use Remote Assistance or similar technologies to share an active session.
>
> **h.** **Media Center Extender.** You may have five Media Center Extender Sessions (or other software or devices which provide similar functionality for a similar purpose) running at the same time to display the software user interface or content on other displays or devices.
>
> **i.** **Electronic Programming Guide.** If the software includes access to an electronic programming guide service that displays customized television listings, a separate service agreement applies to the service. If you do not agree to the terms of the service agreement, you may continue to use the software, but you will not be able to use the electronic programming guide service. The service may contain advertising content and related data, which are received and stored by the software. The service is not available in all areas. Please consult the software information for instructions on accessing the service agreement.
>
> **j.** **Related Media Information.** If you request related media information as part of your playback experience, the data provided to you may not be in your local language. Some countries or regions have laws and regulations which may restrict or limit your ability to access certain types of content.
>
> **k.** **Worldwide Use of the Media Center.** Media Center is not designed for use in every country. For example, although the Media Center information may refer to certain features such as an electronic programming guide or provide information on how to configure a TV tuner, these features may not work in your area. Please refer to the Media Center information for a list of features that may not work in your area.

And he scrolled –

4.   MANDATORY ACTIVATION.
Activation associates the use of the software with a specific computer. During activation, the software will send information about the software and the computer to Gurgle. This information includes the version, language and product key of the software, the Internet protocol address of the computer, and information derived from the hardware configuration of the computer. For more information, see go.Gurgle.com/fwlink/?Linkid=104609. By using the software, you consent to the transmission of this information. If properly licensed, you have the right to use the version of the software installed during the installation process up to the time permitted for activation. **Unless the software is activated, you have no right to use the software after the time permitted for activation.** This is to prevent its unlicensed use. **You are not permitted to bypass or circumvent activation.** If the computer is connected to the Internet, the software may automatically connect to Gurgle for activation. You can also activate the software manually by Internet or telephone. If you do so, Internet and telephone service charges may apply. Some changes to your computer components or the software may require you to reactivate the software. **The software will remind you to activate it until you do.**

5.   VALIDATION.

a.   Validation verifies that the software has been activated and is properly licensed. It also verifies that no unauthorized changes have been made to the validation, licensing, or activation functions of the software. Validation may also check for certain malicious or unauthorized software related to such unauthorized changes. A validation check confirming that you are properly licensed permits you to continue to use the software, certain features of the software or to obtain additional benefits. **You are not permitted to circumvent validation.** This is to prevent unlicensed use of the software. For more information, see go.Gurgle.com/fwlink/?Linkid=104610.

b.   The software will from time to time perform a validation check of the software. The check may be initiated by the software or Gurgle. To enable the activation function and validation checks, the software may from time to time require updates or additional downloads of the validation, licensing or activation functions of the software. The updates or downloads are required for the proper functioning of the software and may be downloaded and installed without further notice to you. During or after a validation check, the software may send information about the software, the computer and the results of the validation check to Gurgle. This information includes, for example, the version and product key of the software, any unauthorized changes made to the validation, licensing or activation functions of the software, any related malicious or unauthorized software found and the Internet protocol address of the computer. Gurgle does not use the information to identify or contact you. By using the software, you consent to the transmission of this information. For more information about validation and what is sent during or after a validation check, see go.Gurgle.com/fwlink/?Linkid=104611.

c.   If, after a validation check, the software is found to be counterfeit, improperly licensed, a non-genuine Gurgle product, or to include unauthorized changes, the functionality and experience of using the software will be affected, for example:
Gurgle may

·   repair the software, remove, quarantine or disable any unauthorized changes that may interfere with the proper use of the software, including circumvention of the activation or validation functions of the software, or

·   check and remove malicious or unauthorized software known to be related to such unauthorized changes, or

·   provide notices that the software is improperly licensed or a non-genuine Gurgle product

And he scrolled –

---

and you may
- receive reminders to obtain a properly licensed copy of the software, or
- need to follow Gurgle's instructions to be licensed to use the software and reactivate, and you may not be able to
- use or continue to use the software or some of the features of the software, or
- obtain certain updates or upgrades from Gurgle

d. You may only obtain updates or upgrades for the software from Gurgle or authorized sources. For more information on obtaining updates from authorized sources see go.Gurgle.com/fwlink/?Linkid=104612.

6. **POTENTIALLY UNWANTED SOFTWARE.** If turned on, Gurgle Defender will search your computer for "spyware," "adware" and other potentially unwanted software. If it finds potentially unwanted software, the software will ask you if you want to ignore, disable (quarantine) or remove it. Any potentially unwanted software rated "high" or "severe," will automatically be removed after scanning unless you change the default setting. Removing or disabling potentially unwanted software may result in
- other software on your computer ceasing to work, or
- your breaching a license to use other software on your computer.

By using this software, it is possible that you will also remove or disable software that is not potentially unwanted software.

7. **INTERNET-BASED SERVICES.** Gurgle provides Internet-based services with the software. It may change or cancel them at any time.

a. **Consent for Internet-Based Services.** The software features described below and in the Gurgle Brass Privacy Statement connect to Gurgle or service provider computer systems over the Internet. In some cases, you will not receive a separate notice when they connect. In some cases, you may switch off these features or not use them. For more information about these features, see the Gurgle Brass Privacy Statement at go.Gurgle.com/fwlink/?linkid=104604. **By using these features, you consent to the transmission of this information.** Gurgle does not use the information to identify or contact you.

Computer Information. The following features use Internet protocols, which send to the appropriate systems computer information, such as your Internet protocol address, the type of operating system, browser and name and version of the software you are using, and the language code of the computer where you installed the software. Gurgle uses this information to make the Internet-based services available to you.

- Plug and Play and Plug and Play Extensions. You may connect new hardware to your computer, either directly or over a network. Your computer may not have the drivers needed to communicate with that hardware. If so, the update feature of the software can obtain the correct driver from Gurgle and install it on your computer. An administrator can disable this update feature.
- Gurgle Update. To enable the proper functioning of the Gurgle Update service in the software (if you use it), updates or downloads to the Gurgle Update service will be required from time to time and downloaded and installed without further notice to you.
- Web Content Features. Features in the software can retrieve related content from Gurgle and provide it to you. Examples of these features are clip art, templates, online training, online assistance and Appshelp. You may choose not to use these web content features.

Digital Certificates. The software uses digital certificates. These digital certificates confirm the identity of Internet users sending X.509 standard encrypted information. They also can be used to digitally sign files and macros, to verify the integrity and origin of the file contents. The software retrieves certificates and updates certificate revocation lists over the Internet, when available.

- Auto Root Update. The Auto Root Update feature updates the list of trusted certificate authorities. You can switch off the Auto Root Update feature.

And he scrolled – ·

- ·Gurgle Media Digital Rights Management. Content owners use Gurgle Media digital rights management technology (WMDRM) to protect their intellectual property, including copyrights. This software and third party software use WMDRM to play and copy WMDRM-protected content. If the software fails to protect the content, content owners may ask Gurgle to revoke the software's ability to use WMDRM to play or copy protected content. Revocation does not affect other content. When you download licenses for protected content, you agree that Gurgle may include a revocation list with the licenses. Content owners may require you to upgrade WMDRM to access their content. Gurgle software that includes WMDRM will ask for your consent prior to the upgrade. If you decline an upgrade, you will not be able to access content that requires the upgrade. You may switch off WMDRM features that access the Internet. When these features are off, you can still play content for which you have a valid license.
- Gurgle Media Player. When you use Gurgle Media Player, it checks with Gurgle for
  - · compatible online music services in your region; and
  - · new versions of the player.
  For more information, go to go.Gurgle.com/fwlink/?Linkid=104605.
- Malicious Software Removal. During setup, if you select "Get important updates for installation", the software may check and remove certain malware from your computer. "Malware" is malicious software. If the software runs, it will remove the Malware listed and updated at www.support.Gurgle.com/?kbid=890830. During a Malware check, a report will be sent to Gurgle with specific information about Malware detected, errors, and other information about your computer. This information is used to improve the software and other Gurgle products and services. No information included in these reports will be used to identify or contact you. You may disable the software's reporting functionality by following the instructions found at www.support.Gurgle.com/?kbid=890830. For more information, read the Gurgle Malicious Software Removal Tool privacy statement at go.Gurgle.com/fwlink/?LinkId=113995.
- Network Awareness. This feature determines whether a system is connected to a network by either passive monitoring of network traffic or active DNS or HTTP queries. The query only transfers standard TCP/IP or DNS information for routing purposes. You can switch off the active query feature through a registry setting.
- Gurgle Time Service. This service synchronizes with time.Gurgle.com once a week to provide your computer with the correct time. You can turn this feature off or choose your preferred time source within the Date and Time Control Panel applet. The connection uses standard NTP protocol.
- IPv6 Network Address Translation (NAT) Traversal service (Teredo). This feature helps existing home Internet gateway devices transition to IPv6. IPv6 is next generation Internet protocol. It helps enable end-to-end connectivity often needed by peer-to-peer applications. To do so, each time you start up the software the Teredo client service will attempt to locate a public Teredo Internet service. It does so by sending a query over the Internet. This query only transfers standard Domain Name Service information to determine if your computer is connected to the Internet and can locate a public Teredo service. If you
  - · use an application that needs IPv6 connectivity or
  - · configure your firewall to always enable IPv6 connectivity
  by default standard Internet Protocol information will be sent to the Teredo service at Gurgle at regular intervals. No other information is sent to Gurgle. You can change this default to use non-Gurgle servers. You can also switch off this feature using a command line utility named "netsh".
- Accelerators. When you click on or move your mouse over an Accelerator in Internet Explorer, any of the following may be sent to the service provider:
  - · the title and full web address or URL of the current webpage,
  - · standard computer information, and
  - · any content you have selected.

And he scrolled –

If you use an Accelerator provided by Gurgle, use of the information sent is subject to the Gurgle Online Privacy Statement. This statement is available at go.Gurgle.com/fwlink/?linkid=31493. If you use an Accelerator provided by a third party, use of the information sent will be subject to the third party's privacy practices.

· <u>Search Suggestions Service</u>. In Internet Explorer, when you type a search query in the Instant Search box or type a question mark (?) before your search term in the Address bar, you will see search suggestions as you type (if supported by your search provider). Everything you type in the Instant Search box or in the Address bar when preceded by a question mark (?) is sent to your search provider as you type. Also, when you press Enter or click the Search button, the text in the Instant Search box or Address bar is sent to the search provider. If you use a Gurgle search provider, use of the information sent is subject to the Gurgle Online Privacy Statement. This statement is available at go.Gurgle.com/fwlink/?linkid=31493. If you use a third-party search provider, use of the information sent will be subject to the third party's privacy practices. You can turn search suggestions off at any time. To do so, use Manage Add-ons under the Tools button in Internet Explorer. For more information about the search suggestions service, see go.Gurgle.com/fwlink/?linkid=128106.

· <u>Consent to Update Infrared Emitter/Receiver</u>. The software may contain technology to ensure proper functioning of the infrared emitter/receiver device shipped with Media Center-based products. You agree that the software may update the firmware of this device.

· <u>Media Center Online Promotions</u>. If you use Media Center features of the software to access Internet-based content or other Internet-based services, such services may obtain the following information from the software to enable you to receive, accept and use certain promotional offers:

    · certain computer information, such as your Internet protocol address, the type of operating system and browser you are using, and the name and version of the software you are using,

    · the requested content, and

    · the language code of the computer where you installed the software.

Your use of the Media Center features to connect to those services serves as your consent to the collection and use of such information.

b. **Use of Information.** Gurgle may use the computer information, accelerator information, search suggestions information, error reports, and Malware reports to improve our software and services. We may also share it with others, such as hardware and software vendors. They may use the information to improve how their products run with Gurgle software.

c. **Misuse of Internet-based Services.** You may not use these services in any way that could harm them or impair anyone else's use of them. You may not use the services to try to gain unauthorized access to any service, data, account or network by any means.

8. **SCOPE OF LICENSE.** The software is licensed, not sold. This agreement only gives you some rights to use the features included in the software edition you licensed. Gurgle reserves all other rights. Unless applicable law gives you more rights despite this limitation, you may use the software only as expressly permitted in this agreement. In doing so, you must comply with any technical limitations in the software that only allow you to use it in certain ways. You may not

    · work around any technical limitations in the software;

    · reverse engineer, decompile or disassemble the software, except and only to the extent that applicable law expressly permits, despite this limitation;

    · use components of the software to run applications not running on the software;

And he scrolled –

> ·   make more copies of the software than specified in this agreement or allowed by applicable law, despite this limitation;
> ·   publish the software for others to copy;
> ·   rent, lease or lend the software; or
> ·   use the software for commercial software hosting services.

Finally, he felt he had read enough. He checked off the box "I have read and understand the terms of the software license," clicked the *purchase* button, and downloaded the software. Then the trouble began.

As soon as he began using the Gurgle Brass software, Melvin found that his original analytical software kept freezing up. Worse yet, when it didn't freeze up, the software seemed to be distorting the presentation of the data. Unsure what was going on, Melvin made a copy of the operating system program and sent it to his Max to download and review it.

Max reported back that, contrary to Melvin's understanding, the program was not designed to interface with his analytical software or his spreadsheet program. Furthermore, the operating system program apparently is designed to run on a desktop computer, not a laptop. Melvin is very upset about this. He is out of pocket $800.00 for the program, and the freezing and distortion of his data has lost him several consulting contracts. He estimates that these contracts were worth $30,000 in fees.

Melvin sent an email to Gurgle complaining about the operating system. He received a reply from Gurgle indicating that he had clicked approval of the license agreement that provided that the program was not designed for the uses for which Melvin used it. Furthermore, Gurgle claimed that Melvin had violated the license agreement by making a copy of the program and sending it to Max.

Questions

A. Melvin realizes that he made a mistake in assuming that the operating system program would interface properly with his analytical software and spreadsheet program. What is the likelihood that this mistake could result in voiding the license agreement?

B. Should Melvin expect to have his $800.00 payment for the operating system restored to him? What about the $30,000 in lost revenue?

C. Could Melvin successfully argue that he already had a contract with Gurgle for the purchase of the operating system program *before* he clicked the purchase button to download the program, because he had already entered and transmitted his credit card payment information, so that the terms of the license did not apply to him?[22]

---

[22] On this issue, recall Chapter 6, *supra*, at 35, n.1.

CHAPTER NINE

DURESS

I. INTRODUCTION

While virtually discredited as a model of contract law,[1] the grand metaphor of a "meeting of the minds" has some resonances in the law of duress as a contract defense. The nuances here are important. To determine whether a contract was formed, we must consider whether each party was "free" to agree or not and if each represented his or her own interests "at arm's length," and whether negotiations led to a joining of their respective interests. In most negotiations, the two parties will not have equal power. Employers generally have stronger power in employment contract negotiations than employees. That inequality alone does not invalidate all employment agreements. The law of duress helps us sort out whether the inequality in bargaining power is sufficient to invalidate the bargain.

What justifies government intervention in an agreement between private parties? We saw one answer to this question in Chapter 4. One of the parties may lack the capacity to enter into a contract. In such situations, we have concerns about the ability of the person to represent his or her own interests because of some weakness or vulnerability.

We saw another justification in the last chapter. There may have been a fundamental mistake, "a belief that is not in accord with the facts,"[2] that either invalidates the apparent bargain or renders it voidable. In other words, in some significant sense the parties spoke past each other and failed to make an agreement about the same subject matter or material terms.

This chapter explores a third reason why a contract may be deemed invalid. In exploring the law or duress, we are challenged to consider whether each party was free to enter into the contract or whether some extraneous factor constrained their power. If I immobilize you and grab your hand, forcing it to scrawl your signature on the bottom line of a contract, there would be little doubt that your assent was not given, and there would be no contract. Similarly, if a man's assent to a bargain was only given because a woman held a pistol to his head, he was not really free to assent at all. But what happens when the power exerted is a degree less intense? What other triggers cause a "yes" to lose the character of freely given assent? What if I threaten your dog? What if I shout at you reasons why you should sign? What if I cry and whine, "How can you do this to me?" What if I say, "Sign, or I'll never offer you this opportunity again"? What if serious financial stress makes someone enter into a bargain he would never normally accept?

---

[1] *See, e.g.*, Farnsworth, *"Meaning" in the Law of Contracts*, 76 Yale L.J. 939, 945 (1967) (criticizing "the metaphor" of "meeting of the minds"). *See generally* Chapter 2, *supra*, at 11 (discussing inadequacy of "meeting of the minds" metaphor).

[2] Rest. (2d) Contracts § 151.

All of these maneuvers share the objective of getting you to enter into a contract with me. Only some of them, presumably, should be tolerated by the law of contract. This chapter explores rules intended to differentiate among various aggressive situations and to determine when we have reached a point, objectively, where the law will no longer tolerate the conduct and recognize an enforceable obligation.

II. OVERVIEW OF THE LAW

Cases of capacity, mistake, and duress often lead to unjust enrichment.[3] In the duress situation, the classic common law statement of the principle was provided by the 1760 case *Mansfield Moses v. Macferlan*,[4] in which Lord Mansfield recognized "imposition," extortion, oppression, and undue advantage as bases for a claim for the return of money paid. As a result, what we now describe as "duress" is actually a varied set of situations in which a contract is forced to a conclusion by inappropriate pressure imposed on one of the parties. "This pressure may take the form of duress by physical compulsion or by threat, or may take the form of undue influence."[5]

The discussion that follows examines the common law principles that apply to compulsion, threat and undue influence. Note that these common law principles are assimilated into the Uniform Commercial Code (UCC), governing contracts for the sale of goods, through UCC § 1–103(b). "Unless displaced by the particular provisions of [the UCC], the principles of law and equity, including . . . the law relative to . . . duress [and] coercion . . . supplement its provisions."[6]

---

[3] Even obscure trial decisions seem to recognize the intuitive proposition linking these types of cases. In *Ridgewood Savings Bank v.Grubb*, 11 Misc.3d 1093, 819 N.Y.S.2d 851 (Queens County Civil Court 2006), a suit between a depositary bank and the payee of a dishonored check, the court made the following observation:

> "Money paid under a mistake of fact may be recovered back, however negligent the party paying may have been in making the mistake, unless the payment has caused such a change in the position of the other party that it would be unjust to require him to refund." (*National Bank of Commerce v. National Mechanics' Banking Assoc.*, 55 N.Y. 211, 213; *Miller v. Schloss*, 218 N.Y. 400, 407 [1916]; *Liberty Mutual Ins. Co. v. Newman*, 92 A.D.2d 613 [2nd Dept.1983]). An action for moneys had and received "lies for *money paid by mistake or an undue advantage taken of the plaintiff's situation.* The gist of this kind of action is that the defendant, upon the circumstances of the case, is obligated by the ties of natural justice and equity to refund the money." *Friar v. Vanguard Holding Corp.*, 78 A.D.2d 83, 88 n. 2 *quoting Mansfield Moses v. Macferlan*, 2 Burr. 1005, 1 Wm Bl 219, 97 Eng. Rep. 676, All Eng. Law Rep. Reprint, 1598– 1774 [1760], 581, 585). *See also Citybank v. Warner*, 113 Misc.2d 749, 750."

(Emphasis added), *quoting Chemical Bank v. Ferst*, N.Y.L.J., Jan. 15, 1991, at 21, col. 2. Similar dynamics are present in *Chiofalo v. Ridgewood Sav. Bank*, 11 Misc.3d 899, 907-908, 816 N.Y.S.2d 324, 330 (Queens County Civil Court 2006).

[4] *Supra* note 3.

[5] REST. (2d) of Contracts, ch. 7 Introductory Note.

[6] UCC § 1-103(b). Comment 2 to UCC § 1–103 provides helpful guidance on what it means to "supplement" UCC provisions:

> . . . [T]he Uniform Commercial Code is the primary source of commercial law rules in areas that it governs, and its rules represent choices made by its drafters and the enacting legislatures about the appropriate policies to be furthered in the transactions it covers. Therefore, while principles of common law and equity may supplement provisions of the Uniform Commercial Code, they may not be used to supplant its provisions, or the purposes and policies those provisions reflect, unless a spe-

A. The Concepts of Duress and Undue Influence

In its most elemental form, duress could involve a person physically compelling a manifestation of assent by the other party – the "forcing your hand" scenario. Clearly, such physical duress is not effective to create a contract.[7] Duress may take the form of a person's[8] improper threat – the "gun to the head" scenario – that forces the other party with no reasonable alternative[9] to assent, and if this is the case the resulting contract is voidable by that party.[10] Problems may remain, however, as to whether or not the threat was serious enough to be improper,[11] and we need to explore that in the next subsection.

---

cific provision of the Uniform Commercial Code provides otherwise. In the absence of such a provision, the Uniform Commercial Code preempts principles of common law and equity that are inconsistent with either its provisions or its purposes and policies.

　　The language of subsection (b) is intended to reflect both the concept of supplementation and the concept of preemption. Some courts, however, had difficulty in applying the identical language of former Section 1-103 to determine when other law appropriately may be applied to supplement the Uniform Commercial Code, and when that law has been displaced by the Code. Some decisions applied other law in situations in which that application, while not inconsistent with the text of any particular provision of the Uniform Commercial Code, clearly was inconsistent with the underlying purposes and policies reflected in the relevant provisions of the Code. *See, e.g., Sheerbonnet, Ltd. v. American Express Bank, Ltd.*, 951 F. Supp. 403 (S.D.N.Y. 1995). In part, this difficulty arose from Comment 1 to former Section 1-103, which stated that "this section indicates the continued applicability to commercial contracts of all supplemental bodies of law except insofar as they are explicitly displaced by this Act." The "explicitly displaced" language of that Comment did not accurately reflect the proper scope of Uniform Commercial Code preemption, which extends to displacement of other law that is inconsistent with the purposes and policies of the Uniform Commercial Code, as well as with its text.

[7] REST. (2d) of Contracts § 174. *See, e.g., Schmidt v. Shah*, 696 F.Supp.2d 44 (D.D.C.2010) (noting that duress by physical compulsion, in contrast to economic duress, rendered contract void rather than voidable).

[8] The person exerting undue force need not be a contracting party to trigger concerns about duress. *Id.* § 175(2). *See, e.g., In re Marriage of Hitchcock*, 265 N.W.2d 599 (Iowa, 1978) (recognizing that duress may be exercised by non-party to contract; holding that trial judge's announcement of views as to what would be just and equitable distribution of assets in a divorce action rendered settlement agreement voidable by wife who was induced to assent to agreement). *Cf. U.S. for Use of Trane Co. v. Bond*, 586 A.2d 734 (Md.1991) (holding that while coercion by husband might render wife's obligation voidable, wife as defendant could not avoid as against innocent third party); *Standard Finance Co., Ltd. v. Ellis*, 657 P.2d 1056 (Hawaii App.1983) (finding that husband of defendant had not induced her to sign document).

[9] On what constitutes a situation in which there is "no reasonable alternative," see REST. (2d) of Contracts § 175, cmt. b.

[10] *Id.* § 175. *See, e.g., Scandinavian Satellite System, AS v. Prime TV Ltd.*, 146 F.Supp.2d 6 (D.D.C. 2001), *reversed* 291 F.3d 839 (D.C.Cir. 2002) (distinguishing duress by threat from duress by physical compulsion). *But see U.S. for Use of Trane Co., supra* (holding that duress sufficient to render contract void consisted not only of actual application of physical force but also threat of immediate physical force sufficient to place person in actual, reasonable, and imminent fear of death, serious personal injury, or actual imprisonment).

[11] *See, e.g. State Bank of Southern Utah v. Troy Hygro Systems*, 894 P.2d 1270 (Utah App.1995) (holding, in collection action for defaulted loans, fact that borrower might have felt some pressure from lending bank did not show sufficient level of coercion to sustain claim of economic duress).

B. Threat as Duress

Undoubtedly, the early common law was rough-hewn enough to look skeptically on any threat that did not suggest immediate bodily harm. Over time, however, courts have become more sympathetic to a wider range of threats considered sufficiently "improper" to call for voiding the contract.[12] Even a threat to one's economic interests may amount to duress.[13] According to the Second Restatement, a threat is improper if:

> (a) what is threatened is a crime or a tort, or the threat itself would be a crime or a tort if it resulted in obtaining property,
> (b) what is threatened is a criminal prosecution,
> (c) what is threatened is the use of civil process and the threat is made in bad faith, or
> (d) the threat is a breach of the duty of good faith and fair dealing under a contract with the recipient.[14]

This suggests that a threat involving behavior that itself is criminal or intentionally wrong would render a resulting contract voidable. In addition, from a more contextual point of view, the Second Restatement considers a threat improper if

> the resulting exchange is not on fair terms, and
> (a) the threatened act would harm the recipient and would not significantly benefit the party making the threat,
> (b) the effectiveness of the threat in inducing the manifestation of assent is significantly increased by prior unfair dealing by the party making the threat, or
> (c) what is threatened is otherwise a use of power for illegitimate ends.[15]

C. Undue Influence as Duress

What if the situation between the two parties is such that as a practical matter an actual threat, express or implied, is not really necessary for one party to command the will of the other party? One party may be very persuasive, capable to close almost any deal, but we would normally expect the other party to hold up their own end of the bargaining

---

[12] *See* REST. (2d) of Contracts § 175, cmt. a, which states in pertinent part:

> Courts originally restricted duress to threats involving loss of life, mayhem or imprisonment, but these restrictions have been greatly relaxed and, in order to constitute duress, the threat need only be improper within the rule stated in § 176.

On what constitutes an "improper" threat under REST. (2d) of Contracts § 176, see text, *infra*, at notes 13-15.

[13] *Jamestown Farmers Elevator, Inc. v. General Mills*, 552 F.2d 1285 (8th Cir. 1977) (recognizing economic distress, here, *inter alia*, shortage of rail cars and threat of higher measure of damages, as basis for possible duress defense). *But cf. Federal Deposit Ins. Corp. v. Meyer*, 755 F.Supp. 10 (D.D.C.1991) (holding that, because defendants' economic duress defense did not involve physical compulsion capable of rendering their signing of promissory notes void, federal banking law barred assertion of that defense against FDIC claim as receiver of failed lending bank); *Standard Finance Co., Ltd. v. Ellis*, 657 P.2d 1056 (Hawaii App.1983) (holding that defense of duress required showing of actual physical force used to compel person to sign agreement).

[14] REST. (2d) of Contracts § 176(1)(a)-(d).

[15] *Id.* § 176(2)(a)-(c).

(or run away). But what if the "persuasiveness" involves exploiting certain emotional or interpersonal pressure points in the other party – knowing how to "push" the other party's "buttons"? At some point, this behavior becomes "[u]ndue influence involv[ing] unfair persuasion, a milder form of pressure than duress."[16] If this undue influence[17] induces the other party to manifest assent, the resulting contract is voidable by the pressured party.[18] If the undue influence is exercised by a third party – *e.g.*, the "mother of the bride" syndrome[19] – the resulting contract is voidable by the other party unless that other party "in good faith and without reason to know of the undue influence either gives value or relies materially on the transaction."[20]

D. Available Remedies

Aside from relatively rare situations involving physical force compelling a party to sign an agreement (which would render the agreement void),[21] duress or undue influence does not create an affirmative cause of action, in tort for example, but instead is viewed as the basis for a contract defense,[22] or an equitable action for avoidance of the contract.[23]

Even in situations where aggressive bargaining or other influence does not arise to the level of duress, the conduct may still affect the availability of other equitable remedies.[24] Thus, if a "contract was induced by . . . unfair practices"[25] or its terms "are otherwise unfair,"[26] then "[s]pecific performance or an injunction will be refused if such relief would be unfair"[27] as a result.

III. PRESSED FOR TIME

This section returns to Melvin C. Witless and his problem with the click-wrapped agreement to purchase the licensed operating system Gurgle Brass.[28] In the events that follow, we consider whether he is being subjected to some form of duress and what his remedy might be if that is the case.

Melvin had gone online to the Gurgle website and clicked on the button to purchase

---

[16] REST. (2d) of Contracts Ch. 7 Topic 2 Introductory Note.

[17] For these purposes, "undue influence" is defined as "unfair persuasion of a party who is under the domination of the person exercising the persuasion or who by virtue of the relation between them is justified in assuming that that person will not act in a manner inconsistent with his welfare." *Id.* § 177(1).

[18] *Id.* § 177(2).

[19] *Cf. Parental Alienation Syndrome Research*, *available at* http://www.mmpi-info.com /psychology-publications-medea-parental-alienation (providing research) (visited Mar. 15, 2014).

[20] REST. (2d) of Contracts § 177(3).

[21] *See Bakos v. Bakos*, 950 So.2d 1257 (Fla.App.2007) (explaining difference between void and voidable contracts; holding prenuptial agreement voidable by wife, but remanding question whether postnuptial agreement was ratification of prenuptial agreement).

[22] *In re Scott*, 481 B.R. 119 (N.D.Ala. 2012).

[23] *Lavoie v. North East Knitting, Inc.*, 918 A.2d 225, 229 (R.I. 2007) (holding undue influence generally only remediable by equitable action for avoidance).

[24] *See* REST. (2d) of Contracts, ch.7 Introductory Note ("misconduct short of that required by [§§ 174-177] may nevertheless be sufficient to preclude equitable relief").

[25] REST. (2d) of Contracts § 364(1)(a).

[26] *Id.* § 364(1)(c).

[27] *Id.* § 364(1).

[28] *See* Chapter 8, *supra*, at 52-59 (setting forth original problem).

the Gurgle Brass operating system. Nothing that he had read on the website suggested that any restrictions applied to the use of his existing software with the new operating system. At the bottom of the page confirming his purchase, he clicked on the following link, http://brass.gurgle.com/en-us/brass1/read-the-gurgle-software-license-terms, to read the terms of the license agreement. Most of the text of that agreement was reproduced in the last chapter. He checked off the box "I have read and understand the terms of the software license," clicked the *purchase* button, and downloaded the software.

As you will recall, since then the operating system program has not worked in the way in which Melvin – perhaps mistakenly – thought it would work.

Assume that Melvin has sent an email to Gurgle complaining about the software and demanding that the license agreement be cancelled and his purchase price be refunded. In response, he received an email from Gurgle Customer Service, which thanked him for his communication, and assured him "that we here at Gurgle are always pleased to hear from one of our fellow adventurers in the Gurgle experience." It then went on as follows:

> We would like to remind you that your use of *Gurgle Brass* is subject to the terms of the License Agreement that you assented to when you placed your order. Please note that your use of *Gurgle Brass* is subject to the Limited Warranty provided in the License Agreement that you assented to. If you have any questions, comments or suggestions concerning this communication, please contact us again. Have a boundary-free day!

Melvin had not read the warranty, as far as he could remember. He went back to the Gurgle website, and finally found a link to the License Agreement. Fortified by a large mug of steaming coffee, he scrolled deep into the License Agreement, and finally came upon the warranty. In fact, he had not reached this point in the agreement last time when he had checked off the box and clicked the purchase button. This is what it said:

> **LIMITED WARRANTY**
>
> A. **LIMITED WARRANTY.** If you follow the instructions and the software is properly licensed, the software will perform substantially as described in the Gurgle materials that you receive in or with the software. Your sole remedy under this warranty is repair or replacement, in Gurgle's sole discretion, of the software.
>
> B. **TERM OF WARRANTY; WARRANTY RECIPIENT; LENGTH OF ANY IMPLIED WARRANTIES. The limited warranty covers the software for one year after acquired by the first user. If you receive supplements, updates, or replacement software during that year, they will be covered for the remainder of the warranty or 30 days, whichever is longer.** If the first user transfers the software, the remainder of the warranty will apply to the recipient. **To the extent permitted by law, any implied warranties, guarantees or conditions last only during the term of the limited warranty.** Some states do not allow limitations on how long an implied warranty lasts, so these limitations may not apply to you. They also might not apply to you because some countries may not allow limitations on how long an implied warranty, guarantee or condition lasts.

> **C.   EXCLUSIONS FROM WARRANTY.** This warranty does not cover problems caused by your
> acts (or failures to act), the acts of others, or events beyond Gurgle's reasonable control.

Melvin sent a second email to Gurgle Customer Service, which read as follows:

> Your program has already ruined my business and cost me $30,000 out of
> pocket. I expect it will end up costing me hundreds of thousands of dollars in
> lost business and repudiated contracts. If you do not cancel this agreement
> and refund me the total purchase price, my first call will be to the *New York
> Times*, my second to *Wired* magazine, and my third to a real red-meat lawyer I
> know. I await your immediate reply.
>
> Have the kind of day you deserve!

The following morning, Melvin received this email from Gurgle's Legal Department:

> Your email has been referred to us by Customer Service. You appear to be
> somewhat dissatisfied with your use of Gurgle Brass, although this appears to
> be the result of the incompatibility of other user software you are operating and
> possibly improper installation of the Gurgle Brass on your part.
>
> We wish to assure you that Gurgle Tech Support is prepared to work with you
> to correct the situation. However, ill-considered remarks are not constructive,
> and we wish to advise you that it is Gurgle's policy to defend its licensing rights
> and its commercial reputation to the full, exhaustive extent of applicable law.
>
> At this time, Gurgle is prepared to offer you the following. Gurgle will cancel the
> current Licensing Agreement and upgrade you to Gurgle Brass Professional,
> for the initial price that you have already paid. In return, Gurgle requires that
> you sign the **Gurgle Brass Pro Licensing Agreement and Claims Waiver**,
> covering a five-year period, by clicking here.
>
> Gurgle believes that this is a generous offer, that it addresses the concerns
> that you have expressed, and that it avoids the necessity of our pursuing all
> appropriate legal remedies that we might otherwise be entitled to in light of
> your email.

Daunted by the prospect of extensive litigation with a large company like Gurgle, Melvin clicked on the Gurgle Brass Pro Licensing Agreement and Claims Waiver, scrolled down to the approval button and clicked it.

Questions

A. Melvin is having second thoughts about signing the Gurgle Brass Pro Licensing Agreement and Claims Waiver. He feels now that he had been intimidated into approving it, and he has come to you for advice.

1. What is the likelihood that you can get this new agreement voided because of Gurgle's apparent intimidation of Melvin?

2. Is there a viable contract claim you could assert to recover the $800.00 that Melvin had originally paid for Gurgle Brass?

3. Does Melvin have potentially sucessful a cause of action for the damages he suffered as a result of using Gurgle Brass?

B. Did Melvin subject *Gurgle* to duress in agreeing to provide him with Gurgle Brass Pro? Could it avoid the new Licensing Agreement?

C. If Melvin had sought your legal advice when he received the email from Gurgle's Legal Department, and then decided to approve the Gurgle Brass Pro Licensing Agreement and Claims Waiver, would that have changed any of your answers to the questions in part A?

CHAPTER TEN

MISREPRESENTATION

I. INTRODUCTION

Does contract law assume that everyone negotiating a contract is a grasping sneak? Reading a classic decision like *Laidlaw v. Organ*,[1] you might reasonably be led to that conclusion. In that case, Organ learned hours before the general population of New Orleans that a British blockade of the city was to be lifted, per the Treaty of Ghent. (In 1814, American forces took a little trip along with Colonel Jackson down the mighty Mississippi and fought the Battle of New Orleans[2] after the treaty had been signed, so this informational asymmetry was obviously widespread at the time.) Once the blockade was lifted, goods like tobacco could be sold to more easily to a larger market and therefore, the lifting of the blockade was bound to cause prices to increase. Armed with this knowledge, Organ purchased a significant quantity of tobacco at an extremely advantageous price from Peter Laidlaw & Co., commission merchants who did not know the blockade was ending. Organ did not lie about the state of affairs in New Orleans, but he did not share the critical information that the blockade would be lifted.[3] Laidlaw later seized the tobacco by force, claiming fraud. Organ sued Laidlaw for the tobacco and tendered the agreed payment price. The jury found for the plaintiff, and judgment was entered ordering return of the tobacco, without damages, "payable as per contract."[4] On a writ of error, the Supreme Court reversed and remanded to the district court for a new trial, because of a faulty jury instruction.[5] However, in dicta Chief Justice John Marshall stated that the buyer was not bound to communicate the secret information to the seller because "[i]t would be difficult to circumscribe the contrary doctrine within proper limits, where the means of intelligence are equally accessible to both parties. But at the same time, each party must take care not to say or do any thing tending to impose upon the other."[6]

We are left with the conclusion that moral aspirations set a higher bar than legal re-

---

[1] 15 U.S. (2 Wheat.) 178 (1817).

[2] *See generally*, Anon. (arr. J. Driftwood), *The Battle of New Orleans* (ca. 1959), *lyrics available at* http://www.metrolyrics.com/the-battle-of-new-orleans-lyrics-johnny-horton.html.

[3] *See Laidlaw*, 15 U.S. at 183-184:

> There [was] no evidence that [Organ] had asserted or suggested any thing to the said Girault[, Laidlaw's employee], calculated to impose upon him with respect to said news, and to induce him to think or believe that it did not exist; and it appearing that the said Girault, when applied to, on the next day, Monday, the 20th of February, 1815, on behalf of [Organ], for an invoice of said tobacco, did not then object to the said sale, but promised to deliver the invoice to the said plaintiff in the course of the forenoon of that day. . . .

[4] Organ had apparently already resold the tobacco to "Boorman and Johnston of the city of New-York." *Laidlaw*, 15 U.S. at 180.

[5] *Id.* at 194.

[6] *Id.*

quirements.[7] Generally, it is legally (if not morally) acceptable to retain crucial information, so long as you do not say or do something to mislead the other party. This principle has a long historical pedigree in the law of contracts. While Chancellor James Kent, in his COMMENTARIES ON AMERICAN LAW, takes a position remarkably similar to that in Marshall's dicta, he contrasts this with more lofty moral rules laid down by Cicero in *de Officiis*,[8] which he argues are of "too severe and elevated a character for practical application, or the cognizance of human tribunals."[9] In the next section, we examine how far the common law is willing to go in policing truthfulness and transparency between parties to a contract.

II. OVERVIEW OF THE LAW

Misrepresentation is treated in the Second Restatement in the same chapter as duress and undue influence.[10] Each of these three concepts involves an imposition on a contracting party by another person, either the other contracting party or perhaps a third party, that raises questions about "the integrity of the bargaining process."[11] Misrepresentation is also related conceptually to mistake,[12] because each of these involves an information deficit or asymmetry that raises questions about the voidability of the resulting contract.[13]

---

[7] Compare the Court's refusal to require one party to share information that would have protected the other party's financial position to the Jewish ethical teaching from a rabbinic text urging business people to "Let your fellow's money be as precious to you as your own." JOSEPH TELUSH-KIN, THE BOOK OF JEWISH VALUES: A DAY TO DAY GUIDE TO ETHICAL LIVING 5 (2000).

[8] Kent describes Cicero's position as follows:

> Cicero . . . states the case of a corn merchant of Alexandria arriving at Rhodes in a time of great scarcity, with a cargo of grain, and with knowledge that a number of other vessels, with similar cargoes, had already sailed from Alexandria for Rhodes, and whom he had passed on the voyage. He then puts the question, whether the Alexandrine merchant was bound in conscience to inform the buyers of that fact, or to keep silence, and sell his wheat for an extravagant price; and he answers it by saying, that, in his opinion, good faith would require of a just and candid man, a frank disclosure of the fact.

2 Kent, *Commentaries on American Law*, Lec. 39, V, n. 85, *available at* http://www.lonang.com/exlibris/kent/kent-39.htm#fn85u.

[9] Kent, *supra*.

[10] REST. (2d) of Contracts ch. 7: Misrepresentation, Duress and Undue Influence.

[11] REST. (2d) of Contracts ch. 7, Introductory Note. Cf. *Germantown Mfg. Co. v. Rawlinson*, 491 A.2d 138 (Pa.Super. 1985) (involving alternative defenses of duress and misrepresentation, as well as unconscionability).

[12] Cf., e.g., *Carpenter v. Vreeman*, 409 N.W.2d 258 (Minn.App. 1987) (involving alternative defenses of mutual mistake and material misrepresentation).

[13] *See* REST. (2d) of Contracts ch. 7, Introductory Note:

> Because a misrepresentation induces the recipient to make a contract while under a mistake, the rules on mistake . . . also apply to many cases of misrepresentation. However, a mistaken party who can show the elements required for avoidance on the ground of misrepresentation will ordinarily prefer to base his claim on this ground rather than attempting to establish the additional elements required by the law of mistake.

On the elements required for a defense of unilateral or mutual mistake, see *supra* at 50-51, text at notes 4-6 (discussing elements of unilateral mistake); 52, text at notes 17-20 (discussing ele-

Not surprisingly, there are some marked similarities between principles applied to misrepresentation and those applied to these other affirmative contract defenses.

The following discussion examines the common law principles that apply to misrepresentation. Note that these common law principles are assimilated into the Uniform Commercial Code (UCC), governing contracts for the sale of goods, through UCC § 1–103(b). "Unless displaced by the particular provisions of [the UCC], the principles of law and equity, including . . . the law relative to . . . fraud [and] misrepresentation . . . supplement its provisions."[14] However, "[s]pecial rules of law" such as "the provisions of the Uniform Commercial Code relating to warranties in contracts for the sale of goods"[15] may supplement or qualify the generally applicable rules discussed by the Second Restatement.[16] Similarly, statutes requiring disclosure in consumer transactions or in transactions in connection with the purchase or sale of securities may qualify generally applicable rules governing misrepresentation.[17]

A. The Concepts of Misrepresentation and Fraud

For purposes of contract law, misrepresentation may be a concern whether or not the misrepresentation involves what, from the perspective of criminal law or torts,[18] would be considered an intentional act of fraud. Contract law focuses on "situations in which a party has been induced to make a contract by a misrepresentation, that is, an assertion, either *fraudulent or non-fraudulent*, that is not in accord with existing facts."[19] Hence, the key concept here is whether or not there has been a *misrepresentation*, defined as "an assertion that is not in accord with the facts."[20]

Having identified a misrepresentation in a contract situation, we must then consider whether or not it should make a difference to our analysis whether the misrepresentation was intentional (*i.e.*, fraudulent) or unintentional (*i.e.*, "innocent"). A further issue is suggested by the facts of *Laidlaw* – whether the absence of a *representation* (mis- or not) about some important fact should make the resulting contract voidable. In other words,

---

ments of mutual mistake). *Compare* REST. (2d) of Contracts §§ 152-153 (concerning elements required for defense of mistake) *and id.* §§ 159-162, 167-169 (concerning elements required for defense of misrepresentation). The difference in required elements of mistake as compared with misrepresentation may be strategic, as where a mistaken belief as to terms of contract unread by plaintiff in final form might still give party a valid defense if the mistake was induced by misrepresentations of the other party. *Sisneros v. Citadel Broadcasting Co.*, 142 P.3d 34 (N.M.App. 2006). *Cf. Adams v. Adams*, 89 P.3d 743 (Alaska 2004), *appeal after remand* 131 P.3d 464 (Alaska 2006) (holding that lessee's substitution of purchase option for right of first refusal clause, without notifying lessor, was material misrepresentation, construing substitution as express and implied assertion that clause was unchanged).

[14] UCC § 1-103(b). Comment 2 to UCC § 1–103 provides helpful guidance on what it means to "supplement" UCC provisions. For the text of comment 2, see Chapter 9, *supra* at 62-63, note 6.

[15] REST. (2d) of Contracts ch. 7, Topic 1, Introductory Note.

[16] *See, e.g.*, UCC § 2-313, official cmt. 8 (concerning affirmations of value or seller's opinion or commendation under subsection § 2-313(2)).

[17] REST. (2d) of Contracts ch. 7, Topic 1, Introductory Note. *See, e.g.*, 15 U.S.C. §§ 77*l*, 78j (providing, under federal securities law, special requirements as to disclosure of material information as to, respectively, sale or purchase and sale of securities).

[18] On liability for misrepresentation under tort law, see REST. (2d) of Torts, chs. 22, 23.

[19] REST. (2d) of Contracts ch. 7, Introductory Note (emphasis added). *See id.* § 179, official cmt. a. ("an assertion need not be fraudulent to be a misrepresentation").

[20] REST. (2d) of Contracts § 159.

when should we treat *concealment* of an important fact[21] or *non-disclosure* of an important fact[22] in the same way as we treat an actual *misrepresentation* of the fact?

The law will treat concealment like an actual misrepresentation when there is action "intended or known to be likely to prevent another from learning a fact."[23] This active concealment is treated as the "equivalent to an assertion that the fact does not exist."[24]

The common law appears to be more skeptical about claims of non-disclosure.[25] The Second Restatement recognizes only four distinct situations in which non-disclosure of a fact would be treated as the equivalent of an active misrepresentation. These are:

> (a) Where [the person aware of the undisclosed fact] knows that disclosure of the fact is necessary to prevent some previous assertion from being a misrepresentation or from being fraudulent or material.
>
> (b) where he knows that disclosure of the fact would correct a mistake of the other party as to a basic assumption on which that party is making the contract and if non-disclosure of the fact amounts to a failure to act in good faith and in accordance with reasonable standards of fair dealing.
>
> (c) where he knows that disclosure of the fact would correct a mistake of the other party as to the contents or effect of a writing, evidencing or embodying an agreement in whole or in part.
>
> (d) where the other person is entitled to know the fact because of a relation of trust and confidence between them.[26]

Even if we are generally disinclined to treat non-disclosure or concealment like an active misrepresentation, we seem to be more willing to do so when the person withholding important information is someone with a fiduciary duty or other special relationship.[27]

B. Required Elements

To render a contract voidable due to misrepresentation, four elements are required to be shown. First, of course, there must be a misrepresentation, either in the form of an affirmative misstatement of fact,[28] an active concealment of a fact,[29] or the non-disclosure of a fact.[30]

---

[21] *Id.* § 160.

[22] *Id.* § 161. Arguably, this was the situation in *Laidlaw* itself.

[23] *Id.* § 160.

[24] *Id. See, e.g., Wells Fargo Bank v. Arizona Laborers, Teamsters and Cement Masons Local No. 395 Pension Trust Fund*, 38 P.3d 12 (Ariz. 2002) (holding there were reasonable inferences from which jury could find fraudulent concealment insofar as bank took measures intended to prevent permanent lender from learning about false information in loans documents).

[25] *See, e.g.,* REST. (2d) of Contracts § 160, cmt. a ("Non-disclosure without concealment is equivalent to a misrepresentation only in special situations.").

[26] REST. (2d) of Contracts § 160(a)-(d). *See, e.g., Spencer v. Barber*, 263 P.3d 296 (N.M. App. 2011) (recognizing that failure to disclose amount of the expected settlement of wrongful-death claim might support one claimant's avoidance of agreement resolving dispute with other claimant).

[27] *See, e.g.,* REST. (2d) of Contracts § 173 (concerning non-disclosure by fiduciary making contract with beneficiary). *Cf. First Nat. Bank & Trust Co. v. Notte*, 293 N.W.2d 530 (Wis. 1980) (noting that relationship of bank and surety would make failure to disclose material information defense to surety obligation).

[28] REST. (2d) of Contracts § 159.

[29] *Id.* § 160.

[30] *Id.* § 161. *Cf. Reed v. King*, 145 Cal.App.3d 261 (Cal.App.1983) (holding that failure by seller and real estate agents to disclose fact that house was site of decade-old multiple murder was

Second, the misrepresentation must either have been fraudulent or involve a material fact.[31] Thus, "an assertion need not be fraudulent to be a misrepresentation. . . . But a misrepresentation that is not fraudulent has no consequences under [REST. (2d) of Contracts Ch. 7] unless it is material."[32] For these purposes, a misrepresentation is fraudulent if the person making the assertion intends the assertion to induce a party to manifest assent, and the person:

> (a) knows or believes that the assertion is not in accord with the facts, or
> (b) does not have the confidence that he states or implies in the truth of the assertion,

or

> (c) knows that he does not have the basis that he states or implies for the assertion.[33]

On the other hand, an assertion is material "if it would be likely to induce a reasonable person to manifest his assent, or if the maker knows that it would be likely to induce the recipient to do so."[34] In any event, the third element required for voidability is that the misrepresentation must have induced the person who receives it to enter into the contract.[35]

Fourth, that person's reliance on the misrepresentation must have been justified.[36] The nature of the assertion that is the subject of the misrepresentation may affect what counts as reasonable reliance.[37] Reliance on someone's assertion of an opinion, for example, is usually not justified, if the assertion is solely one of opinion and does not include a factual assertion beyond the speaker's state of mind.[38] However, where it is rea-

---

material fact that decreased the value of house at time of sale).

[31] REST. (2d) of Contracts § 162. *See, e.g., Kanzmeier v. McCoppin*, 398 N.W.2d 826 (Iowa 1987) (holding negligent omission of information about cattle prices insufficient to make contract voidable for misrepresentation).

[32] REST. (2d) of Contracts § 179, official cmt. a.

[33] *Id.* § 162(1)(a)-(c). *See InterCall, Inc. v. Egenera, Inc.*, 824 N.W.2d 12 (Neb. 2012) (holding that element of fraudulent misrepresentation shown by agent's representations to customer regarding price of provider's services that were made recklessly and without regard to the truth).

[34] REST. (2d) of Contracts § 162(2). *Packard v. KC One, Inc.*, 727 S.W.2d 435 (Mo.App. 1987) (holding materiality to be triable issue unless the statement was so unimportant that reasonable minds could not differ).

[35] REST. (2d) of Contracts § 167. *See, e.g., Jordan v. Knafel*, 880 N.E.2d 1061 (Ill.App. 2007) (holding that fraudulent misrepresentation by lover to professional basketball player as to paternity of her child was material and a substantial factor in inducing player to enter into settlement agreement); *Sarvis v. Vermont State Colleges*, 772 A.2d 494 (Vt. 2001) (holding that teacher's mispresentations as to criminal record and work history induced college into entering into employment contract).

[36] REST. (2d) of Contracts § 168. *See, e.g., First Nat. Bank & Trust Co., supra* (suggesting that surety obligation would be voidable if surety justifiably relied on any fraudulent or material misrepresentation made by the bank to obtain surety's assent); *Carpenter, supra* (holding question whether reliance was justifiable to be question of fact); *Smith v. CSK Auto, Inc.*, 204 P.3d 1001 (Alaska 2009) (holding no justifiable reliance on mistakes regarding identity of employees' physician since employee knew at time of signing waiver agreement who treating physician was).

[37] *See, e.g., Alabi v. DHL Airways, Inc.*, 583 A.2d 1358 (Del.Super. 1990) (finding that material issue of fact existed regarding reasonableness of delivery service's reliance on shipper's description on airway bill of package contents when the shipper twice inquired about availability of large amount of insurance).

[38] REST. (2d) of Contracts § 169. *Cf., e.g., Seybert v. Cominco Alaska Exploration*, 182 P.3d 1079 (Alaska 2008) (remanding to consider whether representations made by insurance adjuster were statements of opinion as to available benefits, and, if so, whether worker reasonably believed that adjuster had special skill or judgment with respect to the subject matter).

sonable to do so, a party receiving an assertion of someone's opinion concerning facts not disclosed and not otherwise known to the party may interpret the opinion as an assertion that (*i*) the facts known to that person are not incompatible with his expressed opinion; or, (*ii*) the person knows facts sufficient to justify him or her in forming it.[39] To the extent that an assertion is simply one of opinion only, however, the party receiving it is *not* justified in relying on it except if he or she

> (a) stands in such a relation of trust and confidence to the person whose opinion is asserted that the recipient is reasonable in relying on it,[40] or
> (b) reasonably believes that, as compared with himself, the person whose opinion is asserted has special skill, judgment or objectivity with respect to the subject matter,[41] or
> (c) is for some other special reason particularly susceptible to a misrepresentation of the type involved.[42]

The Second Restatement also considers the treatment of more specialized issues involving assertions of opinion. Such assertions as to matters of law are subject to the same rules concerning justifiable reliance that apply in the case of other assertions.[43] An assertion of someone's intention[44] does not justify reliance "if in the circumstances a misrepresentation of intention is consistent with reasonable standards of dealing."[45]

---

[39] REST. (2d) of Contracts § 168(2)(a)-(b).

[40] For discussion of the significance of a confidential relationship in justifying reliance on certain opinions, see REST. (2d) of Contracts § 169, cmt. c.

[41] Where special training or experience is necessary to form a reliable judgment, a contract defense might be based on REST. (2d) of Contracts § 168(2) (concerning undisclosed facts). However, if the facts are known to both parties, reliance may have to be justified under the rule stated in § 169(b). *See* REST. (2d) of Contracts § 169, cmt. d.

[42] REST. (2d) of Contracts § 169(a)-(c). Examples of "other special reasons" would include "lack of intelligence, illiteracy, and unusual credulity or gullibility." REST. (2d) of Contracts § 169, cmt. e.

[43] REST. (2d) of Contracts § 170. *See id.* cmt. a:

> Such a statement may or may not be one of opinion. Thus, an assertion that a particular statute has been enacted or repealed or that a particular decision has been rendered by a court is generally not a statement of opinion. The rules that determine the consequences of a misrepresentation of such a matter of law are the same as those that determine the consequences of a similar misrepresentation of any other fact.

As to the treatment of expressed opinions about legal matters, see *id.* cmt. b (explaining application of REST. (2d) of Contracts §§ 167(b), 168(2), and 169 to assertions of opinion about matters of law).

[44] *See* REST. (2d) of Contracts § 171 cmt. a (treating assertion of intention as assertion of fact, *i.e.*, the speaker's state of mind). A promise may also be viewed as a statement of intention as well, namely the promisor's intention to fulfill the promise. REST. (2d) of Contracts § 171 cmt. b (interpreting scope of § 171(2)).

[45] *Id.* § 171(1). Of course, this standard returns us to *Laidlaw* and the psosible expectation that contracting parties are all grasping sneaks. The Second Restatement expresses the issue in the following way:

> A court will take account of all the circumstances, including any usage and the relationship of the parties. A prospective buyer of land may, for example, misrepresent his intended use of the land in order to conceal from the seller some special advantage that the buyer will derive from its purchase, which if known to the seller, would cause him to demand a higher price. The contract is not voidable on this ground if the court concludes that, in all the circumstances, the buyer's misrepresentation is not contrary to reasonable standards of dealing.

C. Available Remedies

A claim of misrepresentation in the formation of a contract is generally not a basis for a claim for damages in contract.[46] In rare cases, however, misrepresentation may prevent the formation of any contract at all.[47] This would be the result if the misrepresentation involved "the character or essential terms of a proposed contract"[48] and induced an apparent manifestation of assent by the party "who neither knows nor has reasonable opportunity to know of the character or essential terms of the proposed contract."[49]

More typically, misrepresentation may make a contract voidable rather than void.[50] If one party's apparent manifestation of assent is induced by a fraudulent or material misrepresentation by the other party "upon which the recipient is justified in relying," then the contract is voidable by the party who receives the misrepresentation.[51] The situation is somewhat more complicated if the source of the misrepresentation is a person who is

---

REST. (2d) of Contracts § 171 cmt. a.

[46] *See, e.g., Massachusetts Housing Opportunities Corp. v. Whitman & Bingham Associates, P.C.,* 983 N.E.2d 734 (Mass.App.Ct. 2013) (holding that misrepresentation could not form basis of affirmative claim for contract damages). *But cf. Abry Partners V, L.P. v. F & W Acquisition LLC,* 891 A.2d 1032 (Del.Ch. 2006) (allowing, in case alleging intentional misrepresentation, claim for rescission).

[47] REST. (2d) of Contracts § 163. *Cf. Massachusetts Housing Opportunities Corp., supra* (noting in dicta that misrepresentation could be basis to hold contract void or prevent formation).

[48] REST. (2d) of Contracts § 163.

[49] *Id.* On "reasonable opportunity to know," see *BankCherokee v. Insignia Development, LLC,* 779 N.W.2d 896 (Minn.App. 2010) (holding that loan guarantor had reasonable opportunity to know what he was signing as individual rather than as corporate guarantor); *Adams, supra* (holding that, since lessor had opportunity to read lease and discover lessee's substitution of purchase option for right of first refusal clause, agreement was voidable, not void); *Indiana Insurance Co. v. Margotte,* 718 N.E.2d 1226 (Ind.App. 1999) (holding settlement agreement with insurer voidable rather than void for fraud, because insured parties had reasonable opportunity to read agreement document but failed to do so). But *cf.* REST. (2d) of Contracts § 172 (establishing rule that **fault of person receiving a misrepresentation, in not knowing or discovering facts before contracting, does not make reliance unjustified, except if failure constitutes "failure to act in good faith and in accordance with reasonable standards of fair dealing").**

The "essential terms" rule generally does not apply to a misrepresentation as to the identity of one party to the proposed contract. REST. (2d) of Contracts § 163, cmt. a. (To similar effect, in the case of a sale of goods, is UCC § 2-403(1)(a).) However, the contract might still be voidable on that basis. REST. (2d) of Contracts § 163, cmt. a., illus. 1, *citing* REST. (2d) of Contracts § 164(1).

[50] REST. (2d) of Contracts § 164. *See, e.g., Adams, supra* (holding that fraudulent substitution in lease of purchase option for right of first refusal clause rendered agreement voidable, not void). For case illustrating interaction with the fraud exception to the Parol Evidence Rule (PER), see *Pacific State Bank v. Greene,* 110 Cal.App.4th 375, 1 Cal.Rptr.3d 739 (Cal.App. 2003) (permitting evidence of lender's factual misrepresentations regarding content of loan documents). On the PER and its application, see Chapter 7, *supra.*

[51] *Id.* § 164(1). *See, e.g., John Hancock Mut. Life Ins. Co. v. Banerji,* 815 N.E.2d 1091 (Mass.App. 2004) (holding that because of insured's material misrepresentation that he had no other insurance coverage, contract for future earnings protection benefits was voidable by insurer). *But cf. Brumley v. Commonwealth Business College Educ. Corp.,* 945 N.E.2d 770 (Ind.App. 2011) (upholding mandatory arbitration clause in enrollment contract despite misrepresentations concerning accreditation of college; noting that, if students' manifestations of assent were induced by fraudulent misrepresentation by college upon which students were justified in relying, contracts were voidable).

not a party to the contract. The contract is still voidable by the person receiving the misrepresentation of the third party, except if the other party to the contract "in good faith and without reason to know of the misrepresentation either gives value or relies materially on the transaction."[52] However, even where a contract was originally voidable because of a misrepresentation, if the facts subsequently come into accord with the assertion *before* notice of an intention to avoid the contract is given by the party who received the misrepresentation, at that point the contract will no longer be voidable.[53] This "curing" rule does not apply if the party has been harmed by reliance on the misrepresentation.[54]

Finally, misrepresentation may be the grounds for a judicial decree reforming the contract.[55] Reformation, within the discretion of the court, is available if the party receiving the misrepresentation "was justified in relying on the misrepresentation."[56] However, reformation is not available "to the extent that rights of third parties such as good faith purchasers for value will be unfairly affected."[57]

III. ROOM SERVICE

Melvin C. Witless was traveling along the Pacific Coast Highway on a long business trip. As the day wore on, he pulled into the parking lot of the West Bestie Hotel and Conference Center, where he had a reservation to break his trip and stay the night. When he made the reservation, he had asked the booking agent on West Bestie's 800 number whether he would be able to access high-speed, secure wifi at the hotel. The agent told him, "Of course, sir, West Bestie is high-tech all the way!"

When he arrived at the hotel, Melvin asked the desk clerk to confirm that wifi access was high-speed and secure. The clerk replied, "Yes, sir. It's state of the art. There is a minimum 24-hour charge of $19.99." Melvin asked if he needed a password to access wifi, and the clerk gave him a card with an ID number and a password for his use in his room. Melvin then gave the clerk his credit card "to cover incidental charges," initialed the check-in form next to the statement "I agree to the terms and conditions for wifi access," and signed the form at the bottom.

When he reached his room, Melvin dropped his bags on the bed, took out his laptop and set it up on the desk. When he got it started and entered the West Bestie website, he

---

[52] *Id.* § 164(2). The UCC applies a similar principle to sales of goods and to negotiable instruments. *See*, respectively, UCC §§ 2-403(1), 3-305 (protecting third party who purchases goods or takes commercial paper for value, in good faith, and without notice of misrepresentation from one who obtained goods or paper from original owner or issuer by means of misrepresentation).

[53] REST. (2d) of Contracts § 165. *But cf. Titan Ins. Co. v. Hyten*, 817 N.W.2d 562 (Mich. 2012) (discussing curing rule, but noting that § 165 had never been adopted by Michigan law).

[54] REST. (2d) of Contracts § 165.

[55] REST. (2d) of Contracts § 166. *See, e.g., NOLM, LLC v. County of Clark*, 100 P.3d 658 (Nev. 2004) (recognizing trend in Nevada case law, Restatement Second of Contracts, and among western states generally to allow reformation of contract where one party knows of mistaken fact in contract for sale of real estate parcels but failed to disclose to other party). For a case holding that this rule is not restricted by the PER, see *Riverisland Cold Storage, Inc. v. Fresno-Madera Production Credit Ass'n*, 291 P.3d 316 (Cal. 2013), *overruling Bank of America etc. Assn. v. Pendergrass*, 48 P.2d 659 (Cal. 1935), and its progeny.

[56] REST. (2d) of Contracts § 166(a). *Cf. Wasser & Winters Co. v. Ritchie Bros. Auctioneers (America), Inc.*, 185 P.3d 73 (Alaska 2008) (upholding reformation of contract sought by defendant who had made innocent misrepresentation).

[57] *Id.* § 166(b).

was confronted with the following page:

Terms of Service

NETWORK USAGE TERMS

These terms and conditions (the "Terms") govern your use of this free internet service. If you do not agree with these Terms, do not use this network.

Links to Third Party Sites

This Website may contain links to other Websites which are not under the control of and are not maintained by this hotel. This hotel is not responsible for the content of those sites. This Hotel is providing these links to you only as a convenience, and the inclusion of any link to such sites does not imply endorsement by this hotel of those sites.

Disclaimer of Warranty

UNLESS OTHERWISE EXPLICITLY STATED, THE MATERIALS ON THE WEBSITE ARE PROVIDED "AS IS", ARE EXPERIMENTAL, AND ARE FOR COMMERCIAL USE ONLY, AND

BEST OF THE WEST /

ALL EXPRESS OR IMPLIED CONDITIONS, REPRESENTATIONS AND WARRANTIES, INCLUDING ANY IMPLIED WARRANTY OF MER-CHANTABILITY, FITNESS FOR A PARTICULAR PURPOSE, OR NON-INFRINGEMENT, ARE DISCLAIMED, EXCEPT TO THE EXTENT THAT SUCH DISCLAIMERS ARE HELD TO BE LEGALLY INVALID. NO REPRESENTATIONS, WARRANTIES OR GUARANTIES AS TO THE QUALITY, SUITABILITY, TRUTH, ACCURACY OR COMPLETENESS OF ANY OF THE MATERIALS CONTAINED ON THE WEBSITE IS IMPLIED. ANY QUESTIONS REGARDING THE MATERIALS SHOULD BE DIRECTED TO THE PROVIDERS OF SUCH MATERIALS.

Limitation of Liability

THIS HOTEL SHALL NOT BE LIABLE FOR ANY DAMAGES SUFFERED AS A RESULT OF USING, MODIFYING, CONTRIBUTING, COPY-ING, DISTRIBUTING, OR DOWNLOADING ANY MATERIALS. IN NO EVENT SHALL THIS HOTEL BE LIABLE FOR ANY INDIRECT, PU-NITIVE, SPECIAL, INCIDENTAL, OR CONSEQUENTIAL DAMAGE (INCLUDING LOSS OF BUSINESS, REVENUE, PROFITS, USE, DATA OR OTHER ECONOMIC ADVANTAGE) HOWEVER IT ARISES, WHETHER FOR BREACH OF CONTRACT OR IN TORT, EVEN IF THIS HOTEL HAS BEEN PREVIOUSLY ADVISED OF THE POSSIBILITY OF SUCH DAMAGE. YOU HAVE SOLE RESPONSIBILITY FOR ADE-QUATE PROTECTION AND BACKUP OF DATA AND/OR EQUIPMENT USED IN CONNECTION WITH THE NETWORK AND WILL NOT MAKE A CLAIM AGAINST THIS HOTEL FOR LOST DATA, RE-RUN TIME, INACCURATE OUTPUT, WORK DELAYS OR LOST PROFITS RESULTING FROM THE USE OF THE MATERIALS. YOU AGREE TO HOLD THIS HOTEL HARMLESS FROM, AND YOU COVENANT NOT TO SUE THIS HOTEL FOR, ANY CLAIMS BASED ON USING THE NETWORK.

U.S. Government Rights

The Materials on this Website are provided with the following restrictions: Use, duplication, or disclosure by the U.S. Government is subject to the re-strictions set forth in the FAR 52.227-19 (June 1987), FAR 52.227-14 (ALT II & ALT III) (June 1987), or if DoD, as specified in DFARS 252.7202-1(a) and 252.7202-3(a) and vendor's applicable license terms, and DFARS 252.227-7013 (Nov 1995) and 252.227-7014(Nov 1995), as applicable. Use of the Materials by the U.S. Government constitutes acknowledgment of this hotel's and/or the Third Party Provider's proprietary rights in them.

General

This Website could include inaccuracies or typographical errors. This hotel and any Third Party Providers may make improvements and/or changes in the products, services, programs, and prices described in this Website at any time without notice. Changes are periodically made to the Website. Any ac-tion related to these Terms will be governed by New Jersey and California law and controlling U.S. federal law. No choice of law rules of any jurisdic-tion will apply. These Terms represent the entire understanding relating to the use of the Website and prevail over any prior or contemporaneous, con-flicting or additional, communications. This hotel can revise these Terms at any time without notice by updating this posting.

 By clicking OK , you accept these terms

West Bestie Hotel and Conference Center 1 Pacific Coast Highway Andalusia, CA 95555-5555

　　Melvin entered his password and clicked on the "OK" link. The wifi Internet connec-tion seemed fine to him. He worked through the night and into the early hours of the morning.

　　Around 3:15 a.m., Melvin prepared to save his work and shut down the connection. However, when he clicked the "Shut Down" button, the following screen message displayed itself to him:

> Thank you for using this service. Total charges **$534.17**
>
> Leave this on your registered credit card?   YES   NO
>
> West Bestie Hotel and Conference Center 1 Pacific Coast Highway Andalusia, CA 95555-5555

Melvin was nonplussed, more than a little perplexed – almost flabbergasted! This was nothing like the 24-hour $19.00 charge he had been told about. He called the Fromnt Desk, but he was put on hold and treated to selections from 1980s elevator music for twenty minutes. He finally hung up and clicked "NO." A new screen message appeared, which said:

> Please contact the Cashier immediately to arrange payment of **$534.17**
>
> In the interim your computer files are frozen.
>
> Enter release code provided by Cashier upon full payment: [   ]
>
> West Bestie Hotel and Conference Center 1 Pacific Coast Highway Andalusia, CA 95555-5555

Melvin discovered that his laptop had frozen, and that he could not access his files. He suspected that the hotel's website had introduced some sort of malware into his computer. He called the Front Desk to complain. The "Hospitality Clerk" explained to him that West Bestie's wifi system automatically reset access fees, and insisted that he had agreed to this when he clicked on the wifi program.

Melvin believes that the hotel staff knew about the reset policy at the time he checked in and didn't warn him although they knew he was going to use the website. Now he is wondering how many other guests West Bestie hotels have treated this way.

Questions

A. Was Melvin the recipient of a misrepresentation by West Bestie Hotel and Conference Center? (Assume for these purposes that West Bestie would be responsible for anything that its employees said to Melvin in their capacity as hotel staff.)

B. If there was a misrepresentation, was it intentional? Fraudulent? What difference would it make to Melvin's situation if it turns out that the misrepresentation was the result of extremely clumsy personnel training by West Bestie's Human Resources Division?

C. What remedies are available to Melvin? Is his agreement to use the wifi program void? Voidable?

D. Melvin read the terms of service – or could have, if he wanted to. What effect does that have on the availability of remedies for Melvin?

CHAPTER ELEVEN

CONDITIONS

I. INTRODUCTION

Conditions are put into contracts to change the nature of a duty or the time of performance duties.[1] Often, a condition states an event that must occur *before* a contractual duty is triggered. This chapter examines the ways in which the law classifies different types of conditions and the way in which those conditions may affect contract duties.

II. OVERVIEW OF THE LAW

Conditions must be future events that are uncertain.[2] At the time the contract is entered, there is some event that may or may not occur. An uncertain event may be a condition even if its occurrence is within the control of one or both of the parties.[3] It may also be an event that is not within the control of either party.[4] If the condition does not happen, the duty tied to it does not arise, and therefore, performance is not due.[5]

Conditions precedent arise before a duty exists.[6] For example, your car insurance company may agree to pay for repairs after an accident if you file a claim within thirty days of the accident. Filing the claim within 30 days is a *condition* that must be met *before* the insurer's duty to pay is triggered. If you do not file your claim within those 30 days, you have not fulfilled the condition that must be met before the company has a duty to pay for your repairs. Filing your claim is what has traditionally been referred to as a "condition precedent,"[7] because it must occur *before* the insurer has a duty to pay for your repairs. (The Second Restatement refers to this simply as a "condition."[8])

Conditions subsequent discharge duties that already exist.[9] For example, a musician

---

[1] JOHN D. CALAMARI & JOSEPH M. PERILLO, THE LAW OF CONTRACTS § 11.2, at 360 (6th ed. 2009).

[2] 13 SAMUEL WILLISTON & RICHARD A. LORD, A TREATISE ON THE LAW OF CONTRACTS § 38:2 (4th ed. 2014).

[3] E. ALLAN FARNSWORTH, CONTRACTS § 8.2, at 504 (4th ed. 2004).

[4] *Id.*

[5] Rest. (2d) Contracts § 224: Condition Defined (1981) ("A condition is an event, not certain to occur, which must occur, unless its non-occurrence is excused, before performance under a contract becomes due.").

[6] 13 SAMUEL WILLISTON & RICHARD A. LORD, A TREATISE ON THE LAW OF CONTRACTS § 38:7 (4th ed. 2014) ("A condition precedent is either an act of a party that must be performed or a certain event that must happen before a contractual right accrues or a contractual duty arises.").

[7] Rest. (1st) Contracts § 250: Definition of "Condition Precedent" and "Condition Subsequent" (1932).

[8] Rest. (2d) Contracts § 224.

[9] JOHN D. CALAMARI & JOSEPH M. PERILLO, THE LAW OF CONTRACTS § 11.7, at 363 (6th ed. 2009).

may have reserved dates to play a concert in an outdoor stadium. He may want to be relieved of the duty to perform if the weather is bad enough to put his band and fans at risk. You may want to structure his contract so that he has a duty to perform but that the duty is discharged if the National Weather Service issues a severe thunderstorm, hurricane or tornado warning. A provision relieving him of his performance duty if such a warning issues was traditionally identified as a "condition subsequent,"[10] because the performer has a duty to play the promised show, but if the weather is dangerous, he will be freed from that obligation.[11]

Because the Second Restatement authors thought the "precedent" and "subsequent" terminology was confusing, they eliminated it.[12] The more modern approach is as follows. If the uncertain event must occur before a duty to perform arises, it is now called simply a condition.[13] An uncertain event that would extinguish a duty after performance is due, is now called a discharge instead of a "condition subsequent."[14] Such an event is not treated under the Second Restatement's rule with respect to conditions, but is covered by the rule applicable to discharge of contractual obligation.[15] Learning the traditional terminology remains important because it appears in foundational contract law decisions. Also, older judges and lawyers still use them. Consequently, some contemporary decisions retain the distinction, even though the court may embrace the Second Restatement for other rules.

A condition is different from a promise because it does not, by itself, create a right or duty.[16] Courts have given contracting parties wide latitude in imposing conditions on the formation or execution of contracts if there is no bad faith or duress present.[17] Because conditions are future events that may or may not occur, satisfaction of the condition is necessary before one can be certain of the contractual obligations.[18]

No exact words are required to create a condition.[19] All that is necessary is an expression that performance is dependent on some other act or event.[20] When interpreting whether a provision is a condition or a promise, words such as "if," "on condition that," "provided that," "subject to," and "in the event of" often signal that a phrase is a condi-

---

[10] Rest. (1st) Contracts § 250.

[11] *See, e.g., Performance Contract*, MARKAMUSIC, www.markamusic.com/pdfs/GenericPerformanceContractOurPA.pdf (last visited Aug. 6, 2014) ("If performance is canceled by sponsor due to inclement weather, acts of God, acts or any other reason, after contractually agreed time of notification of cancellation in favor of rain/snow date, or while performer is traveling to or is already at performance site, sponsor will pay performer in full regardless of whether program described above was never or even partially performed. In the event that a storm should develop while performer is at performance site, performer should decide if cancellation is advisable.").

[12] Rest. (2d) Contracts § 224, Reporter's Note.

[13] Rest. (2d) Contracts § 224.

[14] Rest. (2d) Contracts § 224, cmt. e.

[15] Rest (2d) Contracts § 230.

[16] 13 SAMUEL WILLISTON & RICHARD A. LORD, A TREATISE ON THE LAW OF CONTRACTS § 38:1 (4th ed. 2014).

[17] 13 SAMUEL WILLISTON & RICHARD A. LORD, A TREATISE ON THE LAW OF CONTRACTS § 38:2 (4th ed. 2014).

[18] Rest. (2d) Contracts § 224 cmt. b ("Whether the reason for making an event a condition is to shift to the obligee the risk of its non-occurrence, or whether it is to induce the obligee to cause the event to occur … , there is inherent in the concept of condition some degree of uncertainty as to the occurrence of the event.").

[19] E. ALLAN FARNSWORTH, CONTRACTS § 8.2, at 504 (4th ed. 2004).

[20] 13 SAMUEL WILLISTON & RICHARD A. LORD, A TREATISE ON THE LAW OF CONTRACTS § 38:16 (4th ed. 2014).

tion and not a promise.[21]

III. BOGO LOGO

In this next exercise, you represent a client who wants to hire a designer to create a logo and website for his online volume-buying service. The service identifies vendors and brokers with excess inventory, and buys in bulk–typically at deep discounts of as much as 60 to 80 percent off of the manufacturer's suggested list price. It can then easily turn over the inventory to "club members" on a buy-one-get-one free ("BOGO," an effective member discount of 50 percent off list price) or buy-one-get-one half-price ("BOGO-lite," an effective member discount of 25 percent). You have never represented parties to this type of transaction, so you search online for forms and find the one set forth below:[22]

[YOUR NAME]
[YOUR ADDRESS]

[YOUR TELEPHONE]
[YOUR FAX]
[YOUR EMAIL]

[DATE]

[CLIENT NAME]
[CLIENT TITLE]
[CLIENT COMPANY NAME]
[CLIENT COMPANY ADDRESS]

Project Title/Description: [TITLE] [PROJECT DESCRIPTION]

Confirmation of Engagement: Job No.: [JOB NUMBER]

Schedule: Preliminary Designs: [DATE], Final Design: [DATE]

Copyright Usage: The rights granted to Client are for the usage of the Final Design in its original form only. Client may not modify the Final Design.

License: [EXCLUSIVE / NON_EXCLUSIVE USE]
            [DURATION OF USE]
            [GEOGRAPHIC TERRITORY]
            [MEDIUM OF USE]

---

[21] *Id.* ("Notwithstanding the fact that no particular words are necessary to create a condition, the words 'if' or 'provided,' as well as the phrases 'provided that,' 'on condition that,' 'in the event that,' and other terms that purport to condition performance on another act or event, usually connote an intent for a condition rather than a promise."). *See also* E. ALLAN FARNSWORTH, CONTRACTS § 8.2, at 504 (4th ed. 2004) ("Parties often use language such as "if," "on condition that," "provided that," "in the event that," and "subject to," to make an event a condition but other words may suffice.")

[22] This form is adapted from Jacob C. Myers, *Letter of Agreement*, DESIGN CONTRACTS FOR FREELANCE WEB DESIGNERS, *available at* http://webdesignlaw.com/contracts/letter-of-agreement.html (last visited Aug. 6, 2014).

[**CATEGORY OF USE**].

All other rights to be negotiated separately.

Fee: [FEES]

TERMS

1.   Reservation of Rights: All rights not expressly granted above are retained by the Designer. Any use additional to that expressly granted above requires arrangement for payment of a separate fee.

2.   Revisions: Revisions may be made only by the Designer at the Preliminary Design phase. Additional fees will be charged for revisions made after [**NUMBER OF REVISIONS**] preliminary design revisions, and for additions to project scope.

3.   Payment Schedule: [**UP-FRONT FEE**] upon project commencement, remaining upon project completion.

4.   Payment Terms: Payment due [**NET30 / NET15**] days from issuance of invoice. A one and one half percent (1.5%) monthly service charge will be billed against late payments. Grant of copyright is conditioned upon receipt of final payment, and upon Client's compliance with the terms of this agreement.

5.   Cancellation Fees: In the event of Cancellation, Designer will be compensated for services performed through the date of cancelation in the amount of a prorated portion of the fees due. Upon cancellation all rights to the website revert to the Designer and all original art must be returned, including sketches, comps, or other preliminary materials.

6.   Credits and Promotion: A credit line suitable to the design of the pages will be used. Client agrees to pay an additional fifty percent (50%) of the total fee, excluding expenses, for failure to include credit line. Designer reserves the right to include screen shots of the completed work in his portfolio.

7.   Preliminary Works: Designer retains all rights in and to all Preliminary Designs. Client shall return all Preliminary Designs to Designer within thirty (30) days of completion of the project and all rights in and to any Preliminary Designs shall remain the exclusive property of Designer.

8.   Permissions and Releases: The Client agrees to indemnify and hold the Designer harmless against any and all claims, costs, and expenses, including attorney's fees, due to materials included in the Design at the request of the Client for which no copyright permission or privacy release was requested, or for which uses exceed the uses allowed pursuant to a permission or release.

9.   Miscellaneous: This Agreement shall be binding upon the parties, their heirs, successors, assigns, and personal representatives. This Agreement constitutes the entire understanding of the parties. Its terms can be modified only by a writing signed by both parties, except that the Client may authorize expenses or revisions orally. Any dispute arising out of this agreement will be resolved by negotiation between the parties. If they are unable to resolve the dispute, either party may commence mediation and/ or binding arbitration through the American Arbitration Association. A waiver of a breach of any of the provisions of this Agreement shall not be construed as a continuing waiver of other breaches of the same or other provisions. This Agreement shall be governed by the laws of the State of California and courts of such state shall have exclusive jurisdiction and venue.

This Agreement must be signed and returned before Designer can schedule or begin this job.

Designer Signature: _____

Print Designer Name: _____

Designer Date: _____

Client Signature: _____

Print Client Name: _____

Client Date: _____

Questions

A.   Identify the conditions (practicing use of the terminology of conditions and conditions "precedent" or discharges and conditions "subsequent"), and explain how you know that they are conditions and not promises.

B.   Your client wants to approve the designs before making a final payment. Does this agreement create that right? If not, decide whether a condition or promise is the best way to accomplish that goal, and edit the agreement to meet your client's needs.

CHAPTER TWELVE

IMPOSSIBILITY

I. INTRODUCTION

You cannot squeeze blood from a stone;[1] nor can you get blood from a turnip.[2] These are things that we usually consider to be impossible. (However, apparently you *can* squeeze oil from a stone.[3])

What if two parties enter into a contract requiring one of them to perform an impossible task? Would the contract be enforceable\? If it is, would one party's failure to complete the impossible task lead to a remedy for the other party? Should it make a difference *when* it became evident that the task was impossible? These are the principal questions that contract law seeks to answer when faced with an assertion by one of the parties that its task is impossible.

II. OVERVIEW OF THE LAW

Traditionally, contract law has taken a stark view – some might say a harsh view – of assertions that an obligation may be discharged or avoided because of significant difficulty in its performance.[4] Either it is literally impossible to perform your obligation, or

---

[1] http://idioms.thefreedictionary.com/You+cannot+get+blood+from+a+stone. *See* OXFORD ENGLISH DICTIONARY ONLINE, *blood, to be like getting blood out of (also from) a stone*, http://www.oed.com/view/Entry/20391?redirectedFrom=blood+from+a+stone#eid18099511 ("(originally) to be impossible; (later also in weakened sense) to be extremely difficult"). *But cf.* CAMBRIDGE DICTIONARIES ONLINE http://dictionary.cambridge.org/us/dictionary/british/get-blood-out-of-from-a-stone, which suggests that this is not impossible, merely "extremely difficult" (*e.g.*, "to make someone give or tell you something, when it is extremely difficult because of the character or mood of the person or organization you are dealing with"). This explains, of course, why it is preferable to pursue serious study at Oxford.

[2] *See, e.g.*, F. MARRYAT, JAPHET, IN SEARCH OF A FATHER I. iv. 41 (1836) ("There's no getting blood out of a turnip"). *See also* OXFORD ENGLISH DICTIONARY ONLINE, *blood, supra* (citing Marryat).

[3] This is a relatively new process for both natural gas and oil extraction from shale, an organically rich, fine-grained sedimentary rock. *See* http://www.cleanwateraction.org/feature/fracking-explained.

[4] *Stees v. Leonard*, 20 Minn. 494 (1874) ("If a man bind himself, by a positive, express contract, to do an act in itself possible, he must perform his engagement, unless prevented by the act of God, the law, or the other party to the contract. No hardship, no unforeseen hindrance, no difficulty short of absolute impossibility, will excuse him from doing what he has expressly agreed to do."). The *locus classicus* of this harsh approach is *Paradine v. Jane*, Aleyn 26, [1647] 82 Eng. Rep. 897 (K.B.), described by the U.S. Supreme Court in 1917 as "[t]he seeming absolute confinement to the words of an express contract." *North German Lloyd v. Guaranty Trust Co. of New York*, 244 U.S. 12, 21 (1917) (discussing subsequent "mitigation" of *Paradine* doctrine in situations in which parties would not reasonably have been expected to impose an obligation if they knew of the impossibility). *Paradine* essentially took the view that contract duties were "absolute," in the sense that no

you are bound to perform it. "You cannot walk away from a contract that you can fairly be deemed to have agreed to, merely because performance turns out to be a hardship for you, unless you can squeeze yourself into the impossibility defense or some related doctrine of excuse."[5] As the Seventh Circuit explained,

> [E]ven after you have signed a contract, you are not obliged to become an altruist toward the other party and relax the terms if he gets into trouble in performing his side of the bargain. *Kham & Nate's Shoes No. 2, Inc. v. First Bank*, 908 F.2d 1351, 1357 (7th Cir.1990). Otherwise mere difficulty of performance would excuse a contracting party—which it does not. *Northern Indiana Public Service Co. v. Carbon County Coal Co.*, 799 F.2d 265, 276–78 (7th Cir.1986); *Jennie–O Foods, Inc. v. United States*, 217 Ct.Cl. 314, 580 F.2d 400, 409 (1978) (per curiam); 2 FARNSWORTH ON CONTRACTS, *supra*, § 7.17a, at p. 330.[6]

Hence, mere "hardship" in performance has generally not been a basis for relief from an obligation under the common law. Contract law is particularly hostile to assertions that an obligation should be excused because it has become financially difficult or an economic hardship.[7]

The first great departure from the absolute view of contract duty[8] was *Taylor v. Caldwell*,[9] an 1863 English case in which a service contract required the defendant to make a music hall available to the plaintiffs, and to furnish a band and certain other amusements in connection with plaintiffs' public entertainments. The hall burned down before

Surrey Music Hall, before it burned

---

excuse based on changed circumstances was recognized if not "provided against it in [the] contract." *Paradine* explained that because a party "is to have the advantage of casual profits, so he must run the hazard of casual losses."

[5] *Union Carbide Corp. v. Oscar Mayer Foods Corp.*, 947 F.2d 1333, 1336 (7th Cir. 1991) (dicta, citing *Market Street Associates Limited Partnership v. Frey*, 941 F.2d 588, 594 (7th Cir.1991)).

[6] *Market Street Associates Ltd. Partnership v. Frey*, 941 F.2d 588, 594 (7th Cir. 1991).

[7] *See, e.g., 407 E. 61st St. Garage, Inc. v. Savoy Corp.*, 23 N.Y.2d 275, 281, 296 N.Y.S.2d 338, 344, 244 N.E.2d 37, 41 (Ct. App. 1968):

> [W]here impossibility or difficulty of performance is occasioned only by financial difficulty or economic hardship, even to the extent of insolvency or bankruptcy, performance of a contract is not excused."

(Citations omitted.) In contrast, in certain situations civil law jurisdictions recognize an affirmative, enforceable duty to renegotiate or reform a contract that has become subject to significant hardship – including financial or economic hardship. *See, e.g.*, INSTITUTE FOR THE UNIFICATION OF PRIVATE LAW (UNIDROIT), PRINCIPLES OF INTERNATIONAL COMMERCIAL CONTRACTS §§ 6.2.2-6.2.3 (recognizing duty to renegotiate in situations in which "the occurrence of events fundamentally alters the equilibrium of the contract either because the cost of a party's performance has increased or because the value of the performance a party receives has diminished"). *See generally* JOHN A. SPANOGLE, JR., et al., GLOBAL ISSUES IN CONTRACT LAW ■-■(2d ed., West Academic, 2015) (contrasting impracticability defense and UNIDROIT hardship doctrine).

[8] *See* note **4**, *supra* (discussing absolute view expressed by *Paradine* case).

[9] 1863 WL 6052 (K.B. 1863).

the performance dates, and the plaintiffs sued the defendant for breach of contract. The Court decided the matter in favor of the defendant setting aside the jury verdict for the plaintiff, It found that in the absence of an express contractual provision in allocating such a loss (as would have been required under *Paradine*, presumably), the contract implied a term "that the impossibility of performance arising from the perishing of the person or thing shall excuse performance."

This approach was extended in *Krell v. Henry*,[10] a 1903 Court of Appeal decision, involving a contract to hire a strategically located apartment from which to view the coronation procession of Edward VII in June 1902, at what would otherwise have been a markedly inflated rental price (£75 for two days). The coronation was postponed until August 1902 due to the king's illness, and Krell refused to pay for the apartment. The court found that the rental for the purpose of viewing the procession was so completely the basis of the bargain that its frustration by the postponement rendered the contract without meaning, and relying in part on *Taylor*, the court excused performance. Both *Taylor*[11] and *Krell*[12] have long been assimilated into U.S. law.

King Edward VII

In current contract theory and practice, the law recognizes three basic situations in which some form of relief from contract obligation is available to parties faced with emergent circumstances that interfere significantly with the performance of the contract or its value to the parties. These situations are impossibility, impracticability – a refinement or outgrowth of the impossibility doctrine[13] – and the very distinct doctrine of frus-

---

[10] 1903 WL 12966 (Ct.App. 1903).

[11] *See, e.g., North German Lloyd*, 244 U.S. at 21 (citing *Taylor* as "[f]amiliar example[]"); *Steinbeck v. Steinbeck Heritage Foundation*, --- F.3d ---, 2010 WL 3995982 (2d Cir. 2010) (citing *Taylor* in dispute among John Steinbeck heirs over literary agency agreement); *Opera Co. of Boston, Inc. v. Wolf Trap Foundation for Performing Arts*, 817 F.2d 1094, 1097 (4th Cir.1987) (describing *Taylor* as foundation of doctrine of impossibility in U.S. law).

[12] *See, e.g., La Gloria Oil and Gas Co. v. United States*, 72 Fed.Cl. 544 (Fed.Cl. 2006), *reversed in part sub nom. ConocoPhillips v. United States*, 501 F.3d 1374 (Fed.Cir. 2007) (characterizing *Krell* as "[t]he classic example" of frustration of purpose as a defense that excuses performance on the basis of changed conditions rendering the performance worthless to one of the parties); *Pieper, Inc. v. Land O'Lakes Farmland Feed, LLC*, 390 F.3d 1062, 1066 (8th Cir. 2004) (upholding excuse of performance due to frustration of purpose in contract for purchase of weaner pigs; citing *Krell* as "landmark case on frustration of purpose"); *Waddy v. Riggleman*, 606 S.E.2d 222 (W.Va. 2004) (noting that frustration of purpose originated in English common law and is most frequently attributed to *Krell*); *Ace Securities Corp. Home Equity Loan Trust, Series 2007-HE3 ex rel. HSBC Bank USA, Nat. Ass'n v. DB Structured Products, Inc.*, 5 F.Supp.3d 543 (S.D.N.Y. 2014) (referring to *Krell* as "the leading English case on failure of essential purpose," quoting *Orix Real Estate Capital Mkts., LLC v. Superior Bank, FSB*, 127 F.Supp.2d 981, 983 (N.D.Ill. 2000)); *Edwards v. Leopoldi*, 89 A.2d 264, 268 (N.J.Super. 1952) (noting that "[s]ince the decision in *Krell v. Henry*, . . . the doctrine of frustration has been invoked by the American courts under a variety of circumstances despite the possibility of literal performance of the contract").

[13] *See Transatlantic Financing Corporation v. United States*, 363 F.2d 312, 315 (D.C. Cir. 1966):

> The doctrine of impossibility of performance has gradually been freed from the earlier fictional and unrealistic strictures of such tests as the "implied term" and the parties' "contemplation." Page, *The Development of the Doctrine of Impossibility of Performance*, 18 MICH.L.REV. 589, 596 (1920).

tration of purpose.[14] We examine each of these concepts in turn.

A. Impossibility as a Contract Defense

The fundamental insight that made impossibility of performance an issue in contract law was the principle that "[c]ontract liability is strict liability. . . . The obligor is therefore liable in damages for breach of contract even if he is without fault and even if circumstances have made the contract more burdensome or less desirable than he had anticipated."[15] If there is a risk that the contract obligation may become significantly burdensome, we expect contracting parties to negotiate an allocation of such risk.[16] In the absence of such an allocation, the law generally expects the burdened party to absorb the risk.[17] Over time, however, the defense of strict impossibility has given way to that of "impracticability," or "practical impossibility,"[18] in the sense that

> An extraordinary circumstance may make performance so vitally different from what was reasonably to be expected as to alter the essential nature of that performance. In such a case the court must determine whether justice requires a departure from the general rule that the obligor bear the risk that the contract may become more burdensome or less desirable.[19]

See generally 6 Corbin, Contracts §§ 1320–1372 (rev. ed. 1962); 6 Williston, Contracts §§ 1931–1979 (rev. ed. 1938). It is now recognized that "'A thing is impossible in legal contemplation when it is not practicable; and a thing is impracticable when it can only be done at an excessive and unreasonable cost.'" *Mineral Park Land Co. v. Howard*, 172 Cal. 289, 293, 156 P. 458, 460, L.R.A.1916F, 1 (1916). *Accord, Whelan v. Griffith Consumers Company*, D.C.Mun.App., 170 A.2d 229 (1961). . . .

[14] *See, e.g., Lloyd v. Murphy*, 153 P.2d 47, 53 (Cal. 1944) (noting that "frustration is not a form of impossibility. . . . Performance remains possible but the expected value of performance to the party seeking to be excused has been destroyed by a fortuitous event. . . .").

[15] Rest. (2d) of Contracts, Ch. 11, Introductory Note.

[16] See, e.g., *Great Lakes Gas Transmission Ltd. Partnership v. Essar Steel Minnesota, LLC*, 871 F.Supp.2d 843 (D.Minn. 2012) (holding that difficulty in securing funding to construct steel facility was not basis for claims of impracticability and impossibility where steel manufacturer had failed to condition its performance on obtaining such financing); *Ner Tamid Congregation of North Town v. Krivoruchko*, 638 F.Supp.2d 913, 929 (N.D.Ill. 2009) (holding that absence of financing clause in real estate sales agreement, suggested that financing was not basic assumption of contract; rejecting impossibility and impracticability defenses); *Peoplesoft U.S.A., Inc. v. Softeck, Inc.*, 227 F.Supp.2d 1116 (N.D.Cal. 2002) (holding that, where software licensing contract plainly assigned risk of its customer's noncooperation to licensee, licensee could not avoid liability through frustration of purpose or impracticability defenses).

[17] *Paradine v. Jane, supra* note **4**.

[18] *See, e.g., Record v. Kempe*, 928 A.2d 1199, 1207 (Vt. 2007) (equating "impossibility" with "impracticability" or "practical impossibility"). *See also Allegheny Valley R. Co. v. Urban Redevelopment Authority of City of Pittsburgh*, --- A.3d ---, 2014 WL 2938616 (Commonwealth Court Pa. 2014) (referring throughout to "practical impossibility"); *Kilgore Pavement Maintenance, LLC v. West Jordan City*, 257 P.3d 460 (Utah 2011) (referring consistently to "impracticability/practical impossibility"). *See generally* Rest. (2d) of Contracts, Ch. 11, Reporter's Note (substituting "the term 'impracticability' for 'impossibility' as better expressing the extent of the increased burden that is required"); Rest. (2d) of Contracts, § 261, cmt. d ("Although the rule stated in this Section is sometimes phrased in terms of "impossibility," it has long been recognized that it may operate to discharge a party's duty even though the event has not made performance absolutely impossible. This Section, therefore, uses 'impracticable'").

[19] Rest. (2d) of Contracts, Ch. 11, Introductory Note.

B. Impracticability as a Contract Defense

Historically, the rationale typically given by courts for recognizing the practical impossibility of performance of a contract obligation was their discernment of an "implied term" of the contract that the extraordinary circumstances involved in the case would not occur.[20] The Restatement rejected this rationale "in favor of that of Uniform Commercial Code § 2-615, under which the central inquiry is whether the non-occurrence of the circumstance was a 'basic assumption on which the contract was made.'"[21] In a sense, the circumstances present a case that is simply not covered by the contract, resulting in the discharge of the parties' obligations.[22]

Hence, modern contract law allows a discharge of a party's obligation in situations in which, *after* a contract is made, the party's performance "is made impracticable without his fault by the occurrence of an event the non-occurrence of which was a basic assumption on which the contract was made, . . . unless the language or the circumstances indicate the contrary."[23] This may include, for example, "performance of a duty . . . made impracticable by having to comply with a domestic or foreign governmental regulation or order,"[24] but whatever the event, it must be "supervening," *i.e.*, it must arise after the contract is formed.[25] Furthermore, the event cannot be one that was caused or precipitated by the party claiming discharge.[26] Typically, therefore, the supervening event is external – an "act of God" or action by a third party.[27] "If the event that prevents the obligor's performance is caused by the obligee, it will ordinarily amount to a breach"[28] rather than

---

[20] *Taylor v. Caldwell, supra* note 9.

[21] REST. (2d) of Contracts, Ch. 11, Introductory Note.

[22] *See id.*: "Under the rationale of this Restatement, the obligor is relieved of his duty because the contract, having been made on a different "basic assumption," is regarded as not covering the case that has arisen. It is an omitted case, falling within a 'gap' in the contract."

[23] REST. (2d) of Contracts, § 261.

[24] REST. (2d) of Contracts, § 264. *Cf. White v. J.M. Brown Amusement Co., Inc.*, 601 S.E.2d 342 (S.C. 2004) (holding that local referenda banning video-poker machines, per new legislation, rendered contract giving amusement company exclusive right to place machines in owner's stores impracticable; later decision finding that legislation unconstitutional did not revive contract).

[25] *See, e.g., Massachusetts Bay Transp. Authority v. United States*, 254 F.3d 1367 (Fed. Cir. 2001), *appeal after remand* 167 Fed.Appx. 182 (Fed.Cir.2006) (holding that defendant's contractual obligation to secure insurance endorsements on plaintiff's behalf not excused under doctrine of impossibility, since defendant had reason to know that insurance endorsements were impossible to obtain at the time of contracting). However, situations involving existing, rather than supervening, impracticability may result in discharge of a contractual obligation if the current cause of impracticability is "a fact of which [the party claiming impracticability] has no reason to know." REST. (2d) § 266(1).

[26] *See, e.g., United States v. Winstar Corp.*, 518 U.S. 839 (1996) (holding government liable for breach of contract where change in federal bank regulatory law caused its inability to perform contract); *Westfed Holdings, Inc. v. U.S.*, 52 Fed.Cl. 135 (Ct. Claims 2002) (holding impracticability and frustration of purpose defenses not available to government defendant where government caused change in bank regulatory law that triggered inability to perform contract). *See generally* Michael P. Malloy, *When You Wish Upon* Winstar: *Contract Analysis and the Future of Regulatory Action*, 42 St. Louis U. L.J. 409 (1998) (analyzing impact of *Winstar*).

[27] REST. (2d) of Contracts, § 261, cmt. d. *See Coastal Ventures v. Alsham Plaza, LLC*, 2010 ME 63, 1 A.3d 416 (Me. 2010) (noting that events rendering contract performance impracticable were generally due to either acts of God or acts of third parties).

[28] REST. (2d) of Contracts, § 261, cmt. d.

a discharge.[29]

The "basic assumption" that excludes the supervening event must be one "on which *both* parties made the contract."[30] If a particular person is necessary for the performance of a contractual duty, then the death or incapacity of that person makes the performance impracticable. For example, in a performance contract for a professional sports team, the continued existence of the team is a material assumption of all parties to the contract.[31] Likewise, the existence or nonexistence of an object that is the subject of a contract may be a "basic assumption" the destruction of which triggers impracticability.[32] So, for example, a fire that destroyed timber lands that were the subject of an agreement for harvesting of federally owned timber would be a fundamental change making performance of the contract impracticable.[33]

Otherwise, the "basic" quality required of the assumption usually connotes that the event itself is significant or material, and not a commonplace change of circumstances.[34] The impossibility or impracticability doctrine generally does not justify failure to make a payment required under a contract because of financial distress.[35] For example, an unexpected economic downturn does not make contractual performance "impossible" for purposes of contract law.[36] The fact that the event is foreseeable or foreseen "does not neces-

---

[29] *But cf. Miller v. Mills Const., Inc.*, 352 F.3d 1166, 1172-1173 (8th Cir. 2003) (asserting that contractor's material breach in failing to provide appropriate materials made it "impossible" for subcontractor to perform under contract).

[30] REST. (2d) of Contracts, § 261, cmt. b (emphasis added).

[31] REST. (2d) of Contracts, § 262.

[32] REST. (2d) of Contracts, § 263:

> If the existence of a specific thing is necessary for the performance of a duty, its failure to come into existence, destruction, or such deterioration as makes performance impracticable is an event the non-occurrence of which was a basic assumption on which the contract was made.

See, e.g., Facto v. Pantagis, 915 A.2d 59 (N.J.Super.App.Div.2007) (holding that power failure at banquet hall resulted in impracticability of performance).

[33] *See Spalding & Son, Inc. v. United States*, 28 Fed.Cl. 242 (Ct.Fed.Cl.1993) (When a particular person is hired to perform a task, that person's existence "is an event the non-occurrence of which was a basic assumption on which the contract was made.").

[34] *See* REST. (2d) of Contracts, § 261, cmt. b:

> The continued existence of the person or thing (the non-occurrence of the death of destruction) is ordinarily a basic assumption on which the contract was made, so that death or destruction effects a discharge. . . . The continuation of existing market conditions and of the financial situation of the parties are ordinarily not such assumptions, so that mere market shifts or financial inability do not usually effect discharge under the rule stated in this Section. In borderline cases this criterion is sufficiently flexible to take account of factors that bear on a just allocation of risk.

Not just any death will do, however. *See P.F.I., Inc. v. Kulis*, 363 N.J.Super. 292, 832 A.2d 931 (N.J. Super. 2003) (holding that death of service station owner's husband did not discharge performance of gasoline supply contract as impracticable).

Changes in regulatory provisions that make a party's performance more difficult do not discharge the party. *Prusky v. Reliastar Life Ins. Co.*, 445 F.3d 695 3d Cir. 2006).

[35] *See, e.g., Days Inn of America, Inc. v. Patel*, 88 F.Supp.2d 928 (C.D.Ill. 2000) (in dispute over breach of hotel franchise agreement, rejecting defenses of commercial impossibility, impracticality, and frustration of purpose based on alleged low occupancy caused by a highway closure).

[36] *Hoosier Energy Rural Elec. Co-op. Inc. v. John Hancock Life Ins. Co.*, 582 F.3d 721 (7th Cir. 2009). *See also Ashraf v. Swire Pacific Holdings, Inc.*, 752 F.Supp.2d 1266 (S.D.Fla. 2009) (holding that intervening real estate market crash of 2008 did not support claim of impossibility); *Great Lakes Gas Transmission Ltd. Partnership v. Essar Steel Minnesota, LLC*, 871 F.Supp.2d 843

sarily compel a conclusion that its non-occurrence was not a basic assumption."[37] Hence, the foreseeability of the supervening event demands a case-by-case approach to analysis.[38]

As to language or circumstances that might indicate that discharge is not warranted, contract language of express or implied agreement allocating the risk of an adverse event occurring would result in a party being held liable for damages if the party failed to perform.[39] The "circumstances" that would have a similar effect would the party's "ability to have inserted a provision in the contract expressly shifting the risk of impracticability to the other party."[40] Analysis of the circumstance in this regard is particularly contextual:

> The fact that a supplier has not taken advantage of his opportunity expressly to shift the risk of a shortage in his supply by means of contract language may be regarded as more significant where he is middleman, with a variety of sources of supply and an opportunity to spread the risk among many customers on many transactions by slight adjustment of his prices, than where he is a producer with a limited source of supply, few outlets, and no comparable opportunity. A commercial practice under which a party might be expected to insure or otherwise secure himself against a risk also militates against shifting it to the other party.[41]

C. Frustration of Purpose

In contrast to the close conceptual relationship between impossibility and impracticability,[42] frustration of purpose is a distinctly different doctrine.[43] The Second Restate-

---

(D.Minn. 2012) (holding that global financial crisis, making it difficult to secure funding to construct steel facility, was not a basis for claims of impracticability and impossibility defenses). On the effects of the 2008 crash, see generally MICHAEL P. MALLOY, ANATOMY OF A MELTDOWN (Aspen Publishers, 2010).

[37] REST. (2d) of Contracts, § 261, cmt. b.

[38] *See, e.g.*, REST. (2d) of Contracts, § 261, cmt. c:

> If the supervening event was not reasonably foreseeable when the contract was made, the party claiming discharge can hardly be expected to have provided against its occurrence. However, if it was reasonably foreseeable, or even foreseen, the opposite conclusion does not necessarily follow. Factors such as the practical difficulty of reaching agreement on the myriad of conceivable terms of a complex agreement may excuse a failure to deal with improbable contingencies.

Cf. Lindner v. Meadow Gold Dairies, Inc., 515 F.Supp.2d 1154 (D.Hawaii 2007) (finding that obligation to comply with environmental standards was stated and known obligation and not unforeseeable at the time lease agreement was made); *Sherwin Alumina L.P. v. AluChem, Inc.*, 512 F.Supp.2d 957 (S.D.Tex. 2007) (rejecting commercial impracticability assertion based on state environmental regulations, holding that nonoccurrence of violations not basic assumption on which contract was made).

[39] REST. (2d) of Contracts, § 261, cmt. c.

[40] *Id.* In this regard, Comment c explains:

> This will depend on the extent to which the agreement was standardized (*cf.* § 211), the degree to which the other party supplied the terms (cf. § 206), and, in the case of a particular trade or other group, the frequency with which language so allocating the risk is used in that trade or group (cf. § 219).

Id.

[41] *Id.*

[42] *Cf.* note 18, *supra* (citing cases equating impossibility and impracticability).

ment formulates the frustration of purpose doctrine as follows:

> Where, after a contract is made, a party's principal purpose is substantially frustrated without his fault by the occurrence of an event the non-occurrence of which was a basic assumption on which the contract was made, his remaining duties to render performance are discharged, unless the language or the circumstances indicate the contrary.[44]

This formulation is identical in structure and syntax to the Restatement formulation of the impracticability principle,[45] but it is directed at a situation in which the performance is still possible but is worth substantially less – *i.e.*, is "virtually worthless"[46] – in light of the principal purpose for which the contract was formed in the first place. In other words, in contrast to impracticability, "there is no impediment to performance by either party,"[47] but the incongruity of the performance in relation to the principal purpose makes the contract as unsatisfactory to the party as if it were impracticable to perform.

To mount a successful defense of frustration of purpose leading to the discharge of the frustrated party's remaining obligations, the following elements must be established:

> (1) The frustrated purpose must have been a *principal purpose* of that party in making the contract. "It is not enough that he had in mind some specific object without which he would not have made the contract. The object must be so completely the basis of the contract that, as both parties understand, without it the transaction would make little sense."[48]
>
> (2) The frustration must be *substantial*. "It is not enough that the transaction has become less profitable for the affected party or even that he will sustain a loss. The frustration must be so severe that it is not fairly to be regarded as within the risks that he assumed under the contract."[49]
>
> (3) The frustration must be without the fault of the party who seeks to take ad-

---

[43] *See, e.g., JB Pool Management, LLC v. Four Seasons at Smithville Homeowners Ass'n, Inc.*, 67 A.3d 702 (N.J..App.Div.2013) (distinguishing impossibility and frustration of purpose defenses; rejecting trial court's improper charge to jury on doctrine of frustration of purpose where defendant had asserted impossibility defense). *But cf. BP Chemicals, Inc. v. AEP Texas Cent. Co.*, 198 S.W.3d 449, 460 (Tex.App. 2006) (upholding trial court's finding that utility was excused from performance as result of "commercial impracticability, impossibility of performance, and/or frustration of purpose").

[44] REST. (2d) of Contracts, § 265.

[45] *See supra* text at note 23 (quoting impracticability provision).

[46] REST. (2d) of Contracts, § 265, cmt. a. *See Nye v. Ingersoll Rand Co.*, 783 F.Supp.2d 751, 766 (D.N.J. 2010) (applying "virtually worthless" standard; citing comment a).

[47] REST. (2d) of Contracts, § 265, cmt. a.

[48] *Id. See, e.g., Viking Supply v. National Cart Co., Inc.*, 310 F.3d 1092 (8th Cir. 2002) (excusing manufacturer from further performance of distributorship contract when purpose frustrated by buyer of distributed goods refusing to do business with distributor).

[49] REST. (2d) of Contracts, § 265, cmt. a. *See, e.g., BancorpSouth Bank v. Hazelwood Logistics Center, LLC*, 706 F.3d 888 (8th Cir, 2013) (given real estate loan's stated purpose of remediation and commercial development of property, fact that project might have become less profitable, or that borrower might even sustain a loss, was not sufficient ground to cancel loan contract under frustration doctrine); *Travel Center of Fairfield County, Inc. v. Royal Cruise Line Ltd.*, 154 F.Supp.2d 281 (D.Conn. 2001), *affirmed* 43 Fed.Appx. 461 (2d Cir.2002) (holding that frustration of purpose did not apply to case in which alleged principal purpose was not shared by both parties); *Gander Mountain Co. v. Islip U-Slip LLC*, 923 F.Supp.2d 351 (N.D.N.Y. 2013) (finding that financial difficulty or unprofitability in operating retail store after flooding not substantial for puropses of frustration of purpose).

vantage of the rule.[50]

(4) The *non-occurrence* of the frustrating event must have been a *basic assumption* on which the contract was made.[51] Hence, foreseeability of the event is a factor,[52] "but the mere fact that the event was foreseeable does not compel the conclusion that its non-occurrence was not such a basic assumption."[53]

(5) The rule will not apply "if the language or circumstances indicate the contrary."[54]

Note also that, as with the impracticability defense, the frustration of purpose rule only applies if *supervening* circumstances are involved.[55] Where the performance obligation at issue is simply payment for goods or services already received and enjoyed, the circumstances that trigger frustration of purpose must supervene the *other* party's performance as well.[56] Frustration by circumstances existing at the time of the making of the contract may result in discharge of a contractual obligation if the current cause of frustra-

---

[50] *See, e.g., Far West Fed. Bank v. Thrift Supervision-Director*, 119 F.3d 1358 (9th Cir. 1997) (holding that government defendants' imposition of restrictions on capital of thrift institution was fault that constituted breach of contract, rather than frustration of purpose); *Baker v. Masco Builder Cabinet Group, Inc.*, 912 F.Supp.2d 814 (D.S.D. 2012) (finding that sale of business entirely within employer's control; employer not excused from obligation to pay severance to workers); *Hiriam Hicks, Inc. v. Synagro WWT, LLC*, 867 F.Supp.2d 676, 698-700 (E.D.Pa. 2012) (discussing fault of party claiming frustration of purpose in relation to consultant contract). *But cf. Citgo Petroleum Corp. v. Ranger Enterprises, Inc.*, 632 F.Supp.2d 878 (W.D.Wis. 2009) (finding that breach of one contract by party claiming frustration of purpose with respect to separate but related contract would not be "fault" for purposes of asserting frustration of second contract).

[51] *See, e.g., NPS, LLC v. Ambac Assur. Corp.*, 706 F.Supp.2d 162 (D.Mass. 2010) (finding that decision to enter into financial guarantee insurance policy for certain bonds was not reasonably premised on basic assumption that insurer's credit rating would not be reduced); *Turbines Ltd. v. Transupport, Inc.*, 808 N.W.2d 643 (Neb.App. 2012) (holding that ability to resell and export goods to someone in Asia too generalized to be basic assumption of contract); *Liggett Restaurant Group, Inc. v. City of Pontiac*, 676 N.W.2d 633 (Mich.App.2003), appeal after remand --- N.W.2d ---, 2005 WL 3179679 (Mich.App.2005) (in contract between stadium concessionaire and city and stadium authority, discontinuation by Detroit Lions of use of stadium for home games did not create frustration of purpose where contract expressly provided for possibility that team might miss home games in stadium).

[52] *See, e.g., Lindner v. Meadow Gold Dairies, Inc.*, 515 F.Supp.2d 1154 (D.Hawaii 2007) (holding compliance with Clean Water Act , making tenant's performance under lease more expensive or even unprofitable, did not substantially frustrate purpose of lease; noting that obligation to comply with environmental standards was stated and known obligation and not unforeseeable at the time the agreement was made); *Hiriam Hicks, Inc., supra*, (discussing foreseeability of city's decision to renegotiate contract in relation to asserted frustration of purpose of consultant contract).; *Wheelabrator Environmental Systems, Inc. v. Galante*, 136 F.Supp.2d 21 (D.Conn. 2001) (finding frustration of purpose not available parties foresaw possibility that change in law might affect ability to perform under contract); *Next Gen Capital, L.L.C. v. Consumer Lending Associates, L.L.C.*, 316 P.3d 598 (Ariz.App. 2013) (finding that foreseeability of expiration of statute authorizing lessee's business prevented use of frustration of purpose in relation to lease agreement); *DDS Wireless Intern., Inc. v. Nutmeg Leasing, Inc.*, 75 A.3d 86 (Conn.App. 2013) (holding that because parties foresaw defendant might be dissatisfied with plaintiff's maintenance of taxi-dispatch system and included termination provision in agreement, actual occurrence of dissatisfaction did not excuse defendant's duty to perform its obligations under the agreement).

[53] REST. (2d) of Contracts, § 265, cmt. a.

[54] REST. (2d) of Contracts, § 265, cmt. b.

[55] REST. (2d) of Contracts, § 265, cmt. b.

[56] *Direct Supply, Inc. v. Speciality Hospitals of America, LLC*, 935 F.Supp.2d 137 (D.D.C. 2013).

tion of purpose is "a fact of which [the party claiming impracticability] has no reason to know."[57]

D. Analogous Concepts under UCC Article 2

These common law principles are assimilated into the Uniform Commercial Code (UCC), governing contracts for the sale of goods, to "supplement its provisions."[58] However, UCC Article 2 contains specific provisions that on their own terms offer relief because of changed circumstances.[59] In the simplest situation, the code provides that a contract for sale of goods is "avoided" if goods that are required for performance of the contract suffer a "casualty" without the fault of either party[60] before the "risk of loss" passes to the buyer.[61] The goods must be the only goods that would satisfy the contract – "goods identified when the contract is made"[62] – since otherwise seller could satisfy its obligation by tendering goods other than those destroyed.

The UCC also assimilates the generally applicable common law rule of impracticability of performance under certain specified circumstances. A delay in delivery – or non-delivery in whole or in part – by a seller may not be a breach of a contract for sale of goods if:

> performance as agreed has been made impracticable by the occurrence of a contingency the non-occurrence of which was a basic assumption on which the contract was made or by compliance in good faith with any applicable foreign or domestic governmental regulation or order whether or not it later proves to be invalid.[63]

This excuse is not available if the situation is subject to the substitute performance rule,[64] previously discussed, or when the seller has "assumed a greater obligation."[65] It is

---

[57] REST. (2d) § 266(2). *Cf. Twombly v. Association of Farmworker Opportunity*, 212 F.3d 80 (1st Cir. 2000) (holding that existing law affecting contract not supervening cause of frustration of purpose).

[58] UCC § 1-103(b). Comment 2 to UCC § 1–103 provides helpful guidance on what it means to "supplement" UCC provisions. For the text of comment 2, see Chapter 9, *supra* at 62-63, note 6.

[59] *Cf. International Minerals and Chemical Corp. v. Llano, Inc.*, C.A.10 (N.M.) 1985, 770 F.2d 879 (10th Cir. 1985), *cert. denied*, 475 U.S. 1015 (1986) (viewing both UCC and common law rules on impracticability as default rules in lieu of parties' agreement).

[60] *Beal v. Griffin*, 849 P.2d 118 (Idaho App. 1993). For these purposes, the term *fault* is defined to mean "a default, breach, or wrongful act or omission." UCC §1-201(b)(17). The same result of avoidance would follow, regardless of fault, if the contract contains a "no arrival, no sale" term, *per* UCC § 2-324. UCC § 2-613.

[61] UCC § 2–613(a).

[62] UCC § 2-613. *See Bende and Sons, Inc. v. Crown Recreation, Inc., Kiffe Products Div.*, 548 F.Supp. 1018 (E.D.N.Y. 1982) (holding that identifying goods to contract requires designation of particular or actual goods).

[63] UCC § 2-615(a). This excuse is not available if the seller has assumed a greater obligation or if the UCC provision on substituted performance applies. UCC § 2-615.

[64] *See* UCC § 2-613.

[65] UCC § 2-615. An agreement to assume a greater obligation

> is to be found not only in the expressed terms of the contract but in the circumstances surrounding the contracting, in trade usage and the like. Thus the exemptions of [§ 2-615] do not apply when the contingency in question is sufficiently foreshadowed at the time of contracting to be included among the business risks which are fairly to be regarded as

also unavailable for source-of-supply problems "unless the seller has employed all due measures to assure himself that his source will not fail."[66] Furthermore, availability of this relief is subject to two express conditions:

> (i) If the occurrence of the contingency affects only part of the seller's capacity to perform, seller is required to allocate production and delivery among customers (including regular customers even if not currently under contract), as well as an allocation for seller's own requirements for future manufacture.[67]
>
> (ii) Seller must notify buyer "seasonably" of the delay or non-delivery and, where allocation of production and delivery is required, of the estimated quota that will be made available to buyer.[68]

As with the common law principle, price change alone, even significant price change, would generally not be "a contingency the non-occurrence of which would be a basic assumption" of the contract. The Official Comment to UCC § 2-615 explains:

> Increased cost alone does not excuse performance unless the rise in cost is due to some unforeseen contingency which alters the essential nature of the performance. Neither is a rise or a collapse in the market in itself a justification, for that is exactly the type of business risk which business contracts made at fixed prices are intended to cover. But a severe shortage of raw materials or of supplies due to a contingency such as war, embargo, local crop failure, unforeseen shutdown of major sources of supply or the like, which either causes a marked increase in cost or altogether prevents the seller from securing supplies necessary to his performance is within the contemplation of this section.[69]

The concept of "impracticability" is referenced in another important UCC provision concerning the basic, coordinate contract obligations of delivery and payment. If the agreed method of delivery "becomes commercially impracticable, but a commercially reasonable substitute is available,[70] such substitute performance *must be tendered and accepted.*"[71] Furthermore, if the agreed method of payment fails because of domestic or foreign regulations, seller "may withhold or stop delivery unless the buyer provides a

---

part of the dickered terms, either consciously or as a matter of reasonable, commercial interpretation from the circumstances. . . . The exemption otherwise present through usage of trade . . . may also be expressly negated by the language of the agreement. Generally, express agreements as to exemptions designed to enlarge upon or supplant the provisions of [§ 2-615] are to be read in the light of mercantile sense and reason, for this section itself sets up the commercial standard for normal and reasonable interpretation and provides a minimum beyond which agreement may not go.

UCC § 2-615, Off. Cmt. 8.

[66] UCC § 2-615, Off. Cmt. 5.

[67] UCC § 2-615(b). The provision goes on to explain that seller "may so allocate in any manner which is fair and reasonable." *Id.*

[68] UCC § 2-615(c).

[69] UCC § 2-615, Off. Cmt. 4.

[70] What would constitute a "commercially reasonable substitute" would depend upon "the circumstances, usage of trade or prior course of dealing." UCC § 2-613, Off. Cmt. 1. *Cf. United Equities Co. v. First Nat. City Bank*, 52 A.D.2d 154, *affirmed* 363 N.E.2d 1385 (N.Y.App.Div. 1976) (finding liquidation of contract by crediting buyer with difference between contract price and market price of Japanese yen on delivery date to be commercially reasonable substitute).

[71] UCC § 2-614(1) (emphasis added). Notice that the requirement of a substituted delivery is imposed on *both* the buyer and the seller.

means or manner of payment which is commercially a substantial equivalent."[72] If delivery was already completed, then buyer's payment "by the means or in the manner provided by the regulation" discharges the payment obligation, except in situations in which "the regulation is discriminatory, oppressive or predatory."[73]

The significance of these delivery and payment provisions – in contrast to generally applicable common law rules concerning impracticability[74] – lies in the fact that they concern situations that might not otherwise be viewed as substantially impeding the performance of a contract, though certainly making it more difficult or expensive.[75] These provisions establish clear and generally applicable rules as to the impracticability of delivery and payment.

III. FINISHING THE SPAT

D.P. Wells, the multi-billionaire founder and CEO of the Gurgle Corporation is intent on promoting the operatic career of his wife Susan. Two years ago he hired Giuseppe Cavaletti, a renowned opera coach, to prepare Susan for her debut in the role of Cavalleria Rusticana, the heroine of a newly rediscovered Verdi opera *La Stupida Ricerca*. One year ago, construction was completed on a new opera house in Milan, IL, where Wells expects the world premiere performance of *La Stupida* will take place.

Six months ago, Wells hired his former college roommate Joe "Cotton" Fibre as the drama critic of the GurgleNetNews website. Joe is expected to be part of the team of critics – music, theater, society – who will cover the premiere performance on opening night. The GurgleNetNews Arts and Style Editor has explained to the team that "rave reviews would certainly be appropriate because of the uh historical significance of the uh opera."

Unfortunately, many of those in attendance at the opening night performance found the opera to be unfinished, the orchestra ill-prepared and the performances tremendously disappointing. While

---

[72] UCC § 2-614(2).

[73] *Id.*

[74] *See Hansen-Mueller Co. v. Gau*, 838 N.W.2d 138 (Iowa App. 2013) (discussing difference between application of UCC substitute performance rule and common law impracticability).

[75] *Compare, e.g., International Paper Co. v. Rockefeller*, 161 App.Div. 180, 146 N.Y.S. 371 (1914) (holding contract for sale of spruce to be cut from specified tract of land excused due to fire destroying trees on that tract) *and Meyer v. Sullivan* 723, 181 P. 847 (Cal.App. 1919) (holding contract for delivery of wheat "f.o.b. Kosmos Steamer at Seattle" not excused due to wartime cancellation of sailing schedule). *Cf. Transatlantic Financing Corporation v. United States*, 363 F.2d 312, 315-316 (D.C.Cir. 1966) (Suez Canal closing case, discussing UCC §§ 2-614, 2-615 in dicta).

the GurgleNetNews music and society critics turned in "very positive" reviews of the premiere, Joe was heard to say to the bartender at intermission that it was "impossible to listen to this disaster." He decided to remain at the bar throughout the second, third and fourth acts, because "I can hear as much as I can stand right from here."

Everyone returned to the Gurgle Corporation offices to upload their reviews. When Wells arrived, he told the editor that he wanted to read Joe's review of the dramatic merits of Susan's performance. Wells found Joe impaired and unable to complete inputting his review. He was slumped over his keyboard, and the screen revealed the following incomplete review:

> Susan Wells, a personable but hopelessly incompetent amateur, last night opened the new Gurgle Opera House in a performance of *La Stupida Ricerca* – spuriously attributed to Verdi, but for Verdi's sake I hope not. Her singing, happily, is no concern of this department. Of her acting, it is absolutely impossible tooooooooooooooooooooooooooooooooo

Joe "Cotton" Fibre

Wells slid the keyboard out from under Joe, and he proceeded to the task of completing the review for Joe:

> to say anything except that it appears to represent a new low. The performance, as a whole, was weak and incomprehensible. While it is true that a wealth of training has been expended on the voice of the singer, the result has been pathetic in the extreme, inasmuch as she lacks tonal purity, volume, and the nuances of enunciation so important for a grand opera diva.

When Joe awoke from his slumbers, refreshed and insightful, he found Wells at the computer waiting while the review was being uploaded to the website.

"D.P.," he said with a hint of bemusement, "are we still not speaking to each other?"

"Of course we're speaking to each other, Cotton," Wells replied without lifting his eyes from the screen. "You're fired." Ironically, the drama review under Joe's byline never appeared in GurgleNetNews, because it wasn't completed in time to be uploaded with the rest of the reviews. The opera closed the following day.

Questions

A. You are a new associate with the law firm Dent, Arthur, Dent & Prefect. Joe Fibre has asked the partner with whom you are working whether he has any recourse against Wells and Gurgle Corporation for the termination of his three-year employment contract. The partner has assigned your colleague, Edgar Beaver, to look into the issue of whether inebriation is still a customary condition of employment on a newspaper. She has asked you to examine "whether Joe could claim that his failure to finish the review was excused because of impossibility." What is the likelihood that this argument would prevail if Wells and Gurgle claimed that Joe had breached the employment contract by failing to complete the review?

B. Would it make any difference to your argument if the event that was claimed to make Joe's performance of the contract impossible were the dreadfulness of Susan's performance?

C. Would it make any difference to your argument if the event that was claimed to make Joe's performance of the contract impossible were the fact that he was incapacitated by intermissive libations?

D. Edgar heard about your assignment, and queried, "Couldn't you claim that the purpose of writing the review was frustrated because nobody would believe how bad Susan's performance was?" Explain the situation to your friend Edgar, as politely as you can.

CHAPTER THIRTEEN

WAIVER

I. INTRODUCTION

Parties can plan for many contingencies, but life often brings the unexpected. Sometimes, to make an agreement work as events change, parties are willing to perform even if planned events do or do not occur. For this reason, lawyers who advise clients about contracts frequently face the issue of waiver. Understanding the law of waiver is important in order to guide clients as they face changing circumstances.

II. OVERVIEW OF THE LAW

As we saw in Chapter 10 on conditions, a party's contractual right may be triggered only if a condition occurs. What happens if the party would like to perform even if the required condition does not occur? Sometimes that party may choose to "waive" the occurrence of the condition and act as if it had occurred in order to keep the business relationship intact. A waiver happens when one party excuses the non-occurrence, delay or occurrence of a condition that triggers a contractual right.[1] One leading treatise defines it more succinctly as "a manifestation of willingness to perform despite the nonoccurrence of a condition."[2]

III. THE CURIOUS INCIDENT OF THE DOG

Consider the following example. An apartment rental agreement provides:

> No animals (including mammals, reptiles, birds, fish, rodents, and insects) are allowed, even temporarily, anywhere on the Premises.

The lease further provides:

> any violation of the rental agreement by you, or by your guests, is grounds for terminating the tenancy according to the procedures established by state or local laws.

Tom signed this lease a year ago and has been a model tenant, paying his rent on

---

[1] E. ALLAN FARNSWORTH, CONTRACTS § 8.5, at 524 (4th ed. 2004) (criticizing the frequently used definition of waiver as a "relinquishment of a known right" as "misleading.").

[2] JOSEPH M. PERILLO, CONTRACTS § 11.29 (7th ed. 2013).

time ever since. Over the past few months, Tom was been caring for his father who was stricken with cancer. After his father died, Tom could not bring himself to give away his father's schnauzer. Tom set up the dog's bed in his apartment, hoping the landlord would make an exception to the lease. Adopting the dog violates the rental agreement, and like non-payment of rent, is a condition that triggers the landlord's right to "terminate the tenancy."

So much for the couch . . .

Now that the condition occurred, Lourdes, the landlord, may choose to terminate the lease. She may also decide to continue the agreement and ask Tom to find another home for the dog. But those are not her only two choices. Lourdes may choose to waive the occurrence of this condition. If she does, consider whether she would still have the right to terminate the tenancy for another reason, such as non-payment of rent.

A waiver may be stated expressly or implied by conduct.[3] If Lourdes does not know about the dog, she cannot waive her right under the agreement. But let's imagine that Tom is a forthright young man and asks Lourdes if he can keep the pet. If Lourdes emails Tom, "I am so sorry for your loss, and of course you may adopt your father's dog and keep him here," her message would be an express waiver of the contractual condition triggering her termination right.

If Lourdes never responds to the message but visits the dog, brings her treats, and cares for her while Tom is away interviewing, Lourdes shows – by her conduct—that she has waived the right to terminate the lease.

If you were advising Tom, what would you tell him to do about the dog after his father passes away? Would you recommend that Tom tell Lourdes about his plan to adopt the pet? If you decide to do so, would you advise Tom to send Lourdes a note seeking an express waiver? If so, what would it say? Is there any reason to get the waiver in writing

---

[3] Id. at § 11.31,

even if Lourdes acts with such kindness to Tom's dog? Would your answer change if Lourdes were the apartment manager, and not the landlord?

It is important to understand the difference between a waiver and a modification. Modifications must be made by both parties; waivers may be unilaterally created by one party.[4] Waivers do not require consideration to be valid.[5]

At common law, modifying a contract is just like entering a new one. Modifications require mutual assent, consideration or detrimental reliance, and adherence to any requirement that the agreement be in writing requirement under the state statute of frauds.[6] However, under the UCC, no additional consideration is necessary to modify a contract.[7]

Sometimes, waivers may be retracted. Under the UCC, a waiver may be withdrawn if one party gives the other reasonable notice.[8] However, at common law, some courts hold that a party who disregards a condition is bound "to treat the duty as unconditional."[9] Would that principle affect Tom's lease agreement? Does it change your opinion about whether a waiver or modification is in the best interests of your client?

Questions

A. Victor is hosting a leading privacy law seminar for web designers at a West Bestie hotel. The weekend training session is very competitive, and he is leaving his dog – a magnificent West Highland White Terrier – at home. Hundreds of applicants apply for the 50 slots, and Victor charges a $2500 fee (covering the course, hotel accommodations, and meals) for each accepted participant. Victor must have high speed Internet access for this event. When selecting a host hotel, he always indicates that he will not pay to house and entertain his clients unless the hotel can guarantee it will use its best efforts to provide uninterrupted high speed Internet access during their stay. The hotel assured Victor that its wifi provider can meet his needs. When he arrives at the hotel and inquires about Internet access, the clerk gives him instructions leading him to a website that requires him to sign the wifi agreement from Chapter 10 before he can have Internet access. Will this agreement meet Victor's needs? Should he sign it so he can get online? If not, what would you recommend that he do?

B. Katie Fleming is now the star of the new, fabulously popular break-out television hit *Sugar and Cream*.[10] The tag-line that her character Kay "Sugar" Kandu says in every episode – "I can be sweet . . . and gritty" – is emblazoned on t-shirts all over the world. A little dark cloud has materialized, however. Katie is committed to directing a youth Shakespeare production in the Berkshires in Western Massachusetts this summer, and

---

[4] PERILLO, *supra*, § 11.31.

[5] *See id.* (explaining that "waiver is a very limited exception to the requirement of consideration.")

[6] E. ALLAN FARNSWORTH, CONTRACTS § 8.5 at 524.

[7] UCC § 2-209.

[8] *Id.*

[9] E. ALLAN FARNSWORTH, CONTRACTS § 8.6 at 528.

[10] *See* Chapter 1, *supra*, at 3-10 (discussing the cream in my coffee).

will probably do so every summer during her close friend's tenure as General Manager of the Shakespeare Festival. The producers of *Sugar and Cream* are grumbling that they need her on the set. She says that "Alex knew about this and said it was OK." She also says, "I did it last summer, and he was fine with that!" Alex isn't saying anything, but his lawyers are muttering things like "Paragraph 5.C." and "Paragraph 9." If you were advising Katie, what would you recommend that she do now? Explain the reasons for your advice.

CHAPTER FOURTEEN

BARGAINS AGAINST PUBLIC POLICY

I. INTRODUCTION

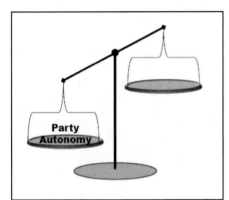

Normally, party autonomy controls contract interpretation and enforcement.

One of the most fundamental principles underlying U.S. contract law is the autonomy of parties to enter freely into contracts. Normally, we expect parties to contract as they wish, and we charge courts with the task of enforcing their agreement without passing judgment on the merits or desirability of the terms. Under certain circumstances, however, Congress, a state legislature or courts may

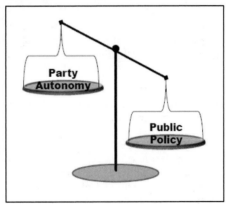

Sometimes, public policy may ouweigh party autonomy.

decide that a public interest outweighs the freedom of contract. In these unusual situations, courts may refuse to enforce a contract term on grounds of public policy. Keep in mind that party autonomy is itself an important public policy. In these cases, the major challenge involves determining *when* the public policy scales tip from weighing decisively in favor of party autonomy and instead favor some other public policy.[1]

---

[1] *See, e.g., Kaufman v. Goldman*, 195 Cal.App.4th 734, 745-746, 124 Cal.Rptr.3d 555, 564 (Cal. App. 2011) (in landlord's suit to enforce settlement agreement with tenant, where tenant raised public policy arguments challenging enforcement of settlement, noting that freedom of contract was an important principle, and that courts should not "blithely apply public policy reasons to void contract provisions"), citing *City of Santa Barbara v. Superior Court*, 41 Cal.4th 747, 161 P.3d 1095 (Cal. 2007), and *VL Systems, Inc. v. Unisen, Inc.*, 152 Cal.App.4th 708, 61 Cal.Rptr.3d 818 (Cal. App. 2007); *MGM Const. Services Corp. v. Travelers Cas. & Sur. Co. of America*, 57 So.3d 884 (Fla. App. 2011) (in contractor suit claiming that subcontract with unlicensed subcontractor was unenforceable, holding that material questions existed as to whether public policy behind licensing ordinance clearly outweighed interest in allowing subcontractor to enforce contractor's promise).

II. OVERVIEW OF THE LAW

A. Contracts and Public Policy

Statutes of frauds represent an internal public policy constraining contracts.

Usually when we talk about public policy in relation to contracts law, we actually mean public policy *extraneous* to contracts law. There are of course public policies *within* contracts law – the principle of party autonomy being the most obvious example. Application of that principle leads to other public policies that may modify the way we apply party autonomy. For example, we have certain rules about required formalities that may limit enforceability even if the parties freely entered the agreement. One example may be seen in Statutes of Frauds requiring some agreements for services or real estate to be in writing.[2] Similarly, UCC § 2-201 sets forth a writings requirement for the sale of goods.[3] Sometimes we think that parties should be required to "put it in writing" or follow formal requirements to give greater certainty to the existence and terms of obligations,[4] or to encourage parties to negotiate until finalize their understanding in writing,[5] or simply to make the parties aware that they are undertaking a serious obligation.[6]

---

[2] *See, e.g.*, REST. (2d) CONTRACTS § 110(1) (identifying types of contracts for which enforcement is forbidden in the absence of written memorandum or applicable exception).

[3] For an example of a traditional justification of the required formalities of UCC § 2-201, see *Joseph E. Seagram & Sons, Inc. v. Shaffer*, C.A.10 (Okla.) 1962, 310 F.2d 668 (10th Cir. 1962), *cert. denied* 373 U.S. 948 (1963) (referring to prevention of fraud and perjury in the enforcement of contract obligations). *But cf. Century Ready-Mix Co. v. Lower & Co.*, 770 P.2d 692, 697 (Wyo.1989) (reflecting modern trend rejecting "rigid adherence" to statute of frauds principle as contrary to philosophy of Uniform Commercial Code "to expand commercial practices through custom and usage as well as by agreement between the parties").

[4] The primary purpose of such statutes is often "assumed to be evidentiary, to provide reliable evidence of the existence and terms of the contract," which may be a significant undertaking and often a complex one. REST. (2d) CONTRACTS, ch.5, Statutory Note.

[5] This is sometimes referred to as the "channeling function" of statutes of frauds. *See Hansen v. Transworld Wireless TV-Spokane, Inc.*, 111 Wash.App. 361, 371, 44 P.3d 929, 935 (Wash. App. 2002) (noting that "parties negotiating complex agreements involving large amounts of money" are "channeled" by requirement into anticipating "that a contract may be made only with a signed writing").

[6] This may be referred to as the "cautionary" or notice purpose of such statutes. "Historical records provide no evidence that the draftsmen had a cautionary purpose, but the Statute serves such a purpose at least in the cases covered by the suretyship and marriage provisions." REST. (2d) CONTRACTS, ch.5, Statutory Note, alluding to REST. (2d) CONTRACTS §§ 110(1)(b), 112 (providing cautionary protection for persons making promises to obliigee of another person); §§ 110(1)(c), 124 (providing cautionary protection for persons making promises upon consideration of marriage).

At least since Holmes' famous excoriation of historical formalities in 1897,[7] principles like the statute of frauds have regularly been criticized as obstructive. We are told that the statute, "never much of a fraud preventer, is no longer used even for the purposes for which its modern-day supporters claim that it should be retained."[8] Nevertheless, this public policy persists,[9] tempered in practice by narrow construction of such statutes[10] and by such principles as estoppel and reasonable reliance.[11]

Another example of a public policy principle *within* contracts law is the set of rules on enforceability of promises against people who might be viewed as more vulnerable in contract negotiations.[12] Still another would be the tangled nest of rules that apply to the enforceable contract rights of "third parties," *i.e.*, anyone other than the two persons we envision in our standard image of negotiating as entering into a contract – *Mr. A* and *Ms. B*. Contracts law allows a third party – someone who is *not* a party to the contract – to enforce

Interests of third parties represent another constraint on party autonomy.

a promise by a contracting party if the third party is an "intended beneficiary" of the contract.[13] Otherwise, a third party is at most an "incidental beneficiary" of a contract, and is

---

[7] Oliver Wendell Holmes, Jr., *The Path of the Law*, 10 HARV. L. REV. 457, 471-473 (1897).

[8] James J. O'Connell, Jr., Comment, *Boats Against the Current: The Courts and the Statute of Frauds*, 47 EMORY L.J. 253, 256 (1998).

[9] For a defence of contract formalities, see Morris G. Shanker, *In Defense of the Sales Statute Of Frauds and Parole [sic] Evidence Rule: A Fair Price of Admission to the Courts*, 100 COM. L.J. 259 (1995).

[10] *See, e.g., K. Miller Const. Co., Inc. v. McGinnis*, 238 Ill.2d 284, 938 N.E.2d 471 (Ill. 2010) (construing statute of frauds applicable to contracts for remodeling work over $1,000; holding that there was no public policy requiring such oral contracts be held unenforceable or that relief in quantum meruit be denied, in light of a subsequent amendment to the statute).

[11] *See, e.g.,* REST. (2d) CONTRACTS §§ 129 (allowing specific performance where action has been taken in reasonable reliance on contract for transfer of interest in land), 139 (allowing, to extent that justice so requires, promise to be enforced by virtue of doctrine of estoppel or by virtue of reliance on promise notwithstanding statute of frauds).

[12] *See* Chapter 4, *supra* (discussing capacity of persons to enter into enforceable contracts).

[13] REST. (2d) CONTRACTS § 304. For these purposes, a third party is considered to be an intended beneficiary

> if recognition of a right to performance in the beneficiary is appropriate to effectuate the intention of the parties and either
>   (a) the performance of the promise will satisfy an obligation of the promisee to pay money to the beneficiary; or
>   (b) the circumstances indicate that the promisee intends to give the beneficiary the benefit of the promised performance.

REST. (2d) CONTRACTS § 302(1)(a)-(b). *See James Family Charitable Foundation v. State Street Bank and Trust Co.*, 80 Mass.App.Ct. 720, 956 N.E.2d 243 (Mass. App. 2011) (recognizing right of foundation that received charitable gift of mutual-fund shares to bring breach of contract action as

not entitled to enforce it.[14]

However, *after* a contract is concluded, we generally allow a contracting party to assign a contract right to a third party, in which "the assignor's right to performance by the obligor is extinguished in whole or in part and the assignee acquires a right to such performance."[15] However, public policy dictates that such an assignment of contractual rights is not permitted if, for example, the assignment would materially prejudice the rights and expectations of the other contracting party.[16]

B. Public Policy Considerations extraneous to Contracts Law

When considering the application of "public policy" to contracts, some may assume that these principles are extraneous to contracts law itself. With respect to the assignment

---

intended beneficiary against bank, as former custodian of the shares, under custodianship agreement between bank and shares' prior owner); *Prouty v. Gores Technology Group*, 121 Cal.App.4th 1225, 18 Cal.Rptr.3d 178 (Cal. App. 2004) (holding that public interest would best be served by interpreting language regarding termination of employees and severance pay in acquisition agreement to accord enforceable rights to former employees against new parent company of former employer).

[14] REST. (2d) CONTRACTS § 315. *Cf. Owner-Operator Independent Drivers Ass'n, Inc. v. Concord EFS, Inc.*, 59 S.W.3d 63 (Tenn. 2001) (holding truck drivers who bought fuel with credit cards were not intended beneficiaries of contract between truck stop operators and bank that issued credit cards).

[15] REST. (2d) CONTRACTS § 317(1). *Cf. City of Hartford v. McKeever*, 139 Conn.App. 277, 55 A.3d 787 (Conn.App. 2012) (discussing extent to which assignee succeeds to obligations of assignor, rather than rights of assignor); *Stenzel v. Dell, Inc.*, 2005 ME 37, 870 A.2d 133 (Me. 2005) (holding seller's assignee was delegated seller's performance obligation). Of course, the contract itself may preclude assignment of rights to a third party. REST. (2d) CONTRACTS § 317(2)(c). *See generally Dick Broadcasting Co., Inc. of Tennessee v. Oak Ridge FM, Inc.*, 395 S.W.3d 653 (Tenn. 2013) (holding consulting agreement to be assignable to prospective purchaser of radio station without consultants' consent, in the absence of limitations in agreement on rights of either party to assign); *Shaffer v. Liberty Life Assur. Co. of Boston*, 319 Ill.App.3d 1048, 746 N.E.2d 285 (Ill. App. 2001) (enforcing anti-assignment provision in tort settlement); *Rumbin v. Utica Mut. Ins. Co.*, 254 Conn. 259, 757 A.2d 526 (Conn. 2000) (construing anti-assignment language in annuity contract).

[16] *See* REST. (2d) CONTRACTS § 317(2)(a), which does not allow an assignment if it

would materially change the duty of the obligor, or materially increase the burden or risk imposed on him by his contract, or materially impair his chance of obtaining return performance, or materially reduce its value to him.

See, e.g., Ruiz v. City of North Las Vegas, 255 P.3d 216 (Nev. 2011) (barring union's assignment to police officer of its right to appeal arbitration decision because, *inter alia*, such assignments could have effect of materially increasing city's bargained-for obligations under collective bargaining agreement); *Dillman v. Town of Hooksett*, 153 N.H. 344, 898 A.2d 505 (N.H. 2006) (same); *Singer Asset Finance Co. v. CGU Life Ins. Co. of America*, 275 Ga. 328, 567 S.E.2d 9 (Ga. 2002) (identifying material reduction in value to obligor, barring assignment of obligee's rights under structured settlement agreement). *But cf. Owen v. CNA Insurance/Continental Cas. Co.*, 167 N.J. 450, 771 A.2d 1208 (N.J. 2001) (holding non-assignment clause in structured settlement agreement unenforceable).

of a contract right to a third party, or any other constraint on assignability, a contract right cannot be assigned if "the assignment is forbidden by statute or is otherwise inoperative on grounds of public policy."[17] This sort of constraint is not unique to the law of assignments. Courts have identified a wide range of "grounds of public policy" that may limit or bar the operation or enforcement of otherwise valid contract provisions. The rest of this section examines typical grounds that are viewed as constraints on freedom of contract and party autonomy.

C. Public Policy Constraints on Contracts Law

Certain public policy principles may render a contract or some provision of the contract unenforceable.[18] Depending upon the relationship among the terms, unenforceability of one provision may make one or more of the other provisions unenforceable as well, or there may be other promises or provisions of the contract that remain operative.[19] While many jurisdictions would view such a public policy argument as an affirmative defense against a contract claim, inconsistency with public policy is the sort of fundamental legal issue that a court conceivably might raise *sua sponte*, although most courts would expect parties to argue the merits of such a question without prompting.[20]

---

[17] REST. (2d) CONTRACTS § 317(2)(b). *See, e.g., HD Supply Facilities Maintenance, Ltd. v. Bymoen*, 125 Nev. 200, 208-211, 210 P.3d 183, 188-190 (Nev. 2009) (Pickering, J., concurring) (in case involving challenged assignment of restrictive covenant in asset sale, providing review and analysis of situtations in which statutory prohibition or public policy constraint would bar assignment); *Burnison v. Johnston*, 277 Neb. 622, 764 N.W.2d 96 (Neb. 2009) (holding that assignment of legal fees owed for previous services not barred as against public policy); *Gurski v. Rosenblum and Filan LLC*, 276 Conn. 257, 885 A.2d 163 (Conn. 2005) (holding public policy barred assignment of legal malpractice claim to adversary in litigation that gave rise to legal-malpractice claim, noting concerns about opportunity and incentive for collusion between assignor and assignee). For an example of a statutory provision limiting recognition of an assignment, see U.C.C. § 5-114(b)-(c), which permits the beneficiary of a letter of credit (L/C) to assign its right to part or all of the proceeds, but does not require the issuer of the L/C to recognize the assignment until it consents to the assignment. However, the issuer's consent "may not be unreasonably withheld if the assignee possesses and exhibits the letter of credit" and presentation of the L/C is properly made to the issuer. UCC § 5-114(d). For analysis of the impact of public policy on the assignment of certain implied warranties, see *Highland Village Partners, L.L.C. v. Bradbury & Stamm Const. Co., Inc.*, 219 Ariz. 147, 195 P.3d 184 (Ariz. App. 2008) (upholding assignments).

[18] Older terminology referred to such contracts or provisions as "illegal," but modern approaches prefer to characterize them as "unenforceable." REST. (2d) CONTRACTS, ch.8, topic 1, Introductory Note. Of course, unenforceability of one provision or term of a contract may result in the unenforceability of other provisions or terms and the denial of any relief to either party. *Id.*

[19] *See, e.g.*, REST. (2d) CONTRACTS § 180 (excusable ignorance of relatively minor facts or legislation on part of promisee but not promisor may result in promisee's claim for damages for breach of the contract).

[20] *See Baugh v. Novak*, 340 S.W.3d 372, 381 (Tenn. 2011) (footnote omitted):

As a general matter, the issues addressed by the appellate courts should be limited to those that have been raised and litigated in the lower courts . . . , and which have been fully briefed and argued in the appellate courts. However, . . . exceptions can be made in appropriate circumstances.

A challenge to the validity of a contract based on public policy grounds is one such exception. One authoritative text has recognized that the issue of whether a contract is contrary to public policy is an issue that trial and appellate courts may raise sua sponte. 15 Grace McLane Giesel, *Corbin on*

Unenforceability on public policy grounds arises from two sources, not always completely distinct.[21] A contract obligation or other term may be unenforceable "if legislation

---

Contracts § 79.6, at 27, 32 (rev. ed. 2003) ("*Corbin on Contracts*"); *see also* Restatement (Second) of Contracts, ch. 8, topic 1, at 5 (1981). We have also previously reached the same conclusion. *Reaves Lumber Co. v. Cain–Hurley Lumber Co.*, 152 Tenn. 339, 344, 279 S.W. 257, 258 (1926) (quoting *Cary–Lombard Lumber Co. v. Thomas*, 92 Tenn. 587, 594, 22 S.W. 743, 745 (1893) (holding that "[t]he courts will deny any relief upon any illegal contract ... whenever the illegality is made to appear")).

We take no issue with the intermediate appellate court's decision to address on its own motion whether the contract between the Baughs and the Novaks was contrary to public policy. However, it would have been better practice for the court to give the parties an opportunity to address this issue before the filing of the opinion. Particularly in cases involving the enforceability of contracts on public policy grounds, fairness dictates providing the parties notice that the court intends to consider the issue and a reasonable opportunity to address the issue before the court decides it. 15 *Corbin on Contracts* § 79.6, at 35.

In addition, questions as to the factual predicates underlying the assertion of public policy grounds for unenforceability may need to be resolved before the public policy principle may be applied. *See, e.g.*, *Austin Bldg. Co. v. Rago, Ltd.*, 63 So.3d 31 (Fla. App. 2011) (holding that genuine issues of material fact existed as to whether general contractor was properly licensed at time subcontractor began working on project; issue was necessary to determine whether construction contract was unenforceable due to unlicensed status of contractor and/or subcontractor).

[21] *See* REST. (2d) CONTRACTS § 178, comment b:

Only infrequently does legislation, on grounds of public policy, provide that a term is unenforceable. When a court reaches that conclusion, it usually does so on the basis of a public policy derived either from its own perception of the need to protect some aspect of the public welfare or from legislation that is relevant to that policy although it says nothing explicitly about unenforceability. . . . In some cases the contravention of public policy is so grave, as when an agreement involves a serious crime or tort, that unenforceability is plain. In other cases the contravention is so trivial . . . that it plainly does not preclude enforcement. In doubtful cases, however, a decision as to enforceability is reached only after a careful balancing, in the light of all the circumstances, of the interest in the enforcement of the particular promise against the policy against the enforcement of such terms.

On the "careful balancing" required in doubtful cases, see notes 24-28 and accompanying text, *infra. See also Oubre v. Entergy Operations, Inc.*, 522 U.S. 422 (1998), *on remand*, 136 F.3d 1342 (5th Cir.1998) (in employment termination agreement, holding that inconsistency with Older Workers Benefit Protection Act rendered release of claims under Age Discrimination in Employment Act unenforceable); *Town of Newton v. Rumery*, 480 U.S. 386 (1987) (holding claims release-charge dismissal plea bargain agreements not unenforceable on public policy grounds); *Martello v. Santana*, 713 F.3d 309 (6th Cir. 2013) (holding that oral and written contracts between attorney and doctor for certain medical/legal consulting work by doctor unenforceable under prohibitions on fee-sharing in Rules of Professional Conduct adopted by Kentucky Supreme Court); *Ritacca v. Girardi*, 996 N.E.2d 236 (Ill. App. 2013) (holding that public policy against medical fee-splitting agreements did not clearly outweigh the interest in enforcing settlement agreement to dissolve medical practice, particularly given law's abhorrence of unjust enrichment of type that would occur here); *Sylver v. Regents Bank, N.A.*, 300 P.3d 718 (Nev. 2013) (holding that public policy of licensing requirement for mortgage bankers did not clearly outweigh interest in enforcing real estate loans); *Jimerson v. Tetlin Native Corp.*, 144 P.3d 470 (Alaska 2006) (holding that settlement agreement involving transfer of shares in native village corporation unenforceable as contravening Alaska Native Claims Settlement Act prohibition on the alienation of shares); *Mayfly Group, Inc. v. Ruiz*, 144 P.3d 1025, 1026-1027 (Or. App. 2006) (holding that, although performance of farm-labor contract violated state licensing statute, violation did not automatically render contract unenforceable

provides that it is unenforceable or the interest in its enforcement is clearly outweighed in the circumstances by a public policy against the enforcement of such terms."[22] Unenforceability based on a statutory provision would depend upon construction of the statutory language in light of legislative intent.[23] The second reason for unenforceability expressly requires a balancing of the interest in enforcing the contract provision (what we have called the public policy of party autonomy) and any public policy against the enforcement of the terms. The factors typically involved in this balancing are as follows. In favor of enforcement, a court would consider:

> (a) the parties' justified expectations,[24]
> (b) any forfeiture that would result if enforcement were denied, and
> (c) any special public interest in the enforcement of the particular term.[25]

In favor of applying the public policy *against* enforcement of the contract provision, a court would consider:

> (a) the strength of that policy as manifested by legislation or judicial decisions,[26]
> (b) the likelihood that a refusal to enforce the term will further that policy,[27]
> (c) the seriousness of any misconduct involved and the extent to which it was de-

---

as contrary to public policy; distinguishing case, as here, involving legislative intent as to enforceability from one in which contract illegality derived from "uncodified public policy").

[22] REST. (2d) CONTRACTS § 178(1). For this purpose, the term "legislation" is understood in a generic sense, including "any fixed text enacted by a body with authority to promulgate rules, including not only statutes, but constitutions and local ordinances, as well as administrative regulations issued pursuant to them. It also encompasses foreign laws to the extent that they are applicable under conflict of laws rules." REST. (2d) CONTRACTS § 178, comment a. *See also* REST. (2d) CONTRACTS § 179(a) ("A public policy against the enforcement of promises or other terms may be derived by the court from . . . legislation relevant to such a policy").

[23] *See, e.g., Mayfly Group, Inc. v. Ruiz*, 144 P.3d 1025, 1026-1027 (Or. App. 2006) (examining legislative intent of farm-labor licensing statute as to enforceability of farm labor agreement); *Griest v. Pennsylvania State University & Dickinson School of Law*, 897 A.2d 1186 (Pa. Super. 2006) (examining public policy behind federal Older Worker's Benefits Protections Act (OWBPA) and finding OWBPA applied only to claims under federal Age Discrimination in Employment Act, and no express statutory provisions in Pennsylvania Human Relations Act prohibiting waiver of claims under state statute in agreement and release employee signed in connection with his resignation).

[24] *See, e.g., Minnesota Fire and Casualty Co. v. Greenfield*, 855 A.2d 854, 866, 871 (Pa. 2004) (holding that, in light of parties' justifiable expectations when entering into homeowners policy, obligation of insurer to defend or indemnify homeowner for wrongful death of houseguest, who allegedly overdosed on heroin sold to guest by homeowner, was not enforceable).

[25] REST. (2d) CONTRACTS § 178(2)(a)-(c).

[26] This is considered a critical factor in the "careful balancing." *See* REST. (2d) CONTRACTS § 178, comment c:

> Even when the policy is one manifested by legislation, it may be too insubstantial to outweigh the interest in the enforcement of the term in question. . . . A disparity between a relatively modest criminal sanction provided by the legislature and a much larger forfeiture that will result if enforcement of the promise is refused may suggest that the policy is not substantial enough to justify the refusal.

[27] On the relationship between the contract term in question and the public policy, see REST. (2d) CONTRACTS § 178, comment d.

liberate, and
    (d) the directness of the connection between that misconduct and the term.[28]

Where the promisee has substantially performed, enforcement of a promise is generally not precluded on public policy grounds because of some improper use that the promisor intended to make of what he obtained from the promisee.[29] Alternatively, if a contract can be apportioned into corresponding pairs of part performances properly regarded as agreed equivalents[30] and one pair is not offensive to public policy, that part of the contract will be enforceable by the party who did not engage in serious misconduct.[31]

In a contract in which there is only one promise, or only one that raises public policy concerns,[32] the unenforceabilty of the promise may be the end of the inquiry, although unenforceability of that one promise may raise issues concerning available remedies for the other contracting party.[33] Where there is an exchange of promises, and public policy renders one of them unenforceable, one must then decide whether the other promise (*i*) remains an enforceable obligation, or (*ii*) is also constrained by the public policy directly or indirectly, or (*iii*) is otherwise subject to an affirmative defense such as impossibility, impracticability, or frustration of purpose,[34] or (*iv*) is not required to be performed, be-

---

[28] REST. (2d) CONTRACTS § 178(3)(a)-(d). For commentary on the "other factors" mentioned in paragraphs (c) and (d), see REST. (2d) CONTRACTS § 178, comment e.

[29] REST. (2d) CONTRACTS § 182. However, enforcement of the promise *will* be barred if

    (a) acted for the purpose of furthering the improper use, or
    (b) knew of the use and the use involves grave social harm.

REST. (2d) CONTRACTS § 182(a)-(b). *See, e.g., Zenon v. R.E. Yeagher Management Corporation*, 748 A.2d 900 (Conn. App. 2000) (holding promissory note unenforceable, because its execution was integral to illegal transfer of lessor's liquor license to lessees).

[30] On this application of the concept of "divisibility" or "severability" of pairs of part performances, see REST. (2d) CONTRACTS § 183, comment a. *See also* REST. (2d) CONTRACTS § 184, comment a (discussing partial enforcement in the absence of ability to apportion under § 183). *Cf. Papageorge v. Banks*, 81 A.3d 311, 320 n.11 (D.C. App. 2013) (holding that portion of agreement not itself offensive to public policy was unenforceable as essential part of agreed exchange), quoting REST. (2d) CONTRACTS § 184(1).

[31] REST. (2d) CONTRACTS § 183. *See, e.g., Booker v. Robert Half Intern., Inc.*, 413 F.3d 77 (D.C.Cir. 2005) (severing arbitration agreement's unenforceable bar on punitive damages while enforcing remainder of agreement); *Sanford v. Sanford*, 694 N.W.2d 283 (S.D. 2005) (declaring provisions in prenuptial agreement purporting to limit or waive spousal support to be void as contrary to public policy, and severing them from valid portions of the agreement), *Swain v. Auto Services, Inc.*, 128 S.W.3d 103 (Mo. App. 2003) (severing unenforceable venue provision of vehicle service contract from general agreement to arbitrate).

[32] *See, e.g.*, REST. (2d) CONTRACTS § 184 (treating only part of the term as unenforceable; allowing enforcement of remainder by party who did not engage in serious misconduct).

[33] *See, e.g.*, REST. (2d) CONTRACTS § 178, comment f (discussing effect of unenforceability of one provision on other provisions and on available remedies).

[34] *See* Chapter 12, *supra* (discussing impossibility and related concepts providing affirmative defenses). *Cf. Gaddy Engineering Co. v. Bowles Rice McDavid Graff & Love, LLP*, 746 S.E.2d 568 (W.Va. 2013) (holding fee-sharing agreement between engineering company/expert consultant and lawyer and law firm unenforceable due to impracticability caused by changed circumstances, not

cause the unenforceable promise was a condition for the other promise.[35]

D. Typical Public Policy Grounds for Unenforceability

Certain situations seem to be typical examples of public policy disputes over the enforceability of contracts. The following material highlights these situations. However, you should note that public policy arguments are context-sensitive and may arise in any contract dispute that invites the "careful balancing"[36] of the interest in party autonomy and constraining public policy.

1. Statutory Mandates

"A public policy against the enforcement of promises or other terms may be derived by the court from . . . legislation relevant to such a policy."[37] The role of statutes as a source of public policy has been referred to in the preceding discussion.[38] The modern role of legislation as a source of public policy constraints should not be underestimated.[39]

2. Restraint of Trade

"A promise is unenforceable on grounds of public policy if it is unreasonably in restraint of trade."[40] Certain types of restraints of trade are prohibited by federal antitrust law,[41] another statutory source of a constraining public policy. Beyond this, however, public policy against the enforcement of promises or other contract terms may also be derived by a court from "the need to protect some aspect of the public welfare, as is the

---

reaching issue of unenforceability due to public policy against such fee-sharing agreements).

[35] *See* Chapter 11, *supra* (discussing conditions and their effects on other promises). However, To the extent that a contract provision requiring the occurrence of a condition is unenforceable as against applicable public policy, "a court may excuse the non-occurrence of the condition unless its occurrence was an essential part of the agreed exchange." REST. (2d) CONTRACTS § 185. *See Hill v. American Family Mut. Ins. Co.*, 249 P.3d 812 (Idaho 2011) (holding that term in auto insurance contract requiring insured to exhaust tortfeasor's bodily-injury policy as a condition for claiming underinsured-motorist benefits was unenforceable condition for public-policy reasons; nonoccurrence of condition could be excused unless its occurrence was an essential part of the insurance contract).

[36] REST. (2d) CONTRACTS § 178, comment b.

[37] REST. (2d) CONTRACTS § 179(a).

[38] *See* text and accompanying notes 22-23, *supra*.

[39] *See* REST. (2d) CONTRACTS § 179, comment b ("declaration of public policy has now become largely the province of legislators rather than judges").

[40] REST. (2d) CONTRACTS § 186(1). For these purposes, a promise "is in restraint of trade if its performance would limit competition in any business or restrict the promisor in the exercise of a gainful occupation." REST. (2d) CONTRACTS § 186(2).

[41] *See, e.g.*, 15 U.S.C. §§ 1-2 (Sherman Act prohibitions on, *inter alia*, certain restraints of trade). *See also id.* § 18 (Clayton Act prohibitions on, *inter alia*, certain acquisitions that may have effect of substantially lessening competition or of tending to create monopoly). *See generally* ELEANOR M FOX & DANIEL A CRANE, GLOBAL ISSUES IN ANTITRUST AND COMPETITION LAW (West Academic, 2010) (providing introduction to antitrust law in comparative perspective).

case for the judicial policies against . . . restraint of trade."[42] So, for example, a "no-hire" provision in a service contract between a physical-therapist agency and a health-care provider that operated nursing homes, which restricted the employment opportunities of employees without their knowledge and consent, could constitute an unreasonable restraint of trade in contravention of state public policy, and thus be unenforceable.[43]

Reasonable restrictions on post-contract competition generally do not trigger these public policy concerns.[44] However, where the non-competition agreement imposes a restraint that is not ancillary to an otherwise valid transaction or relationship like employment,[45] the agreement is likely to be considered unreasonably in restraint of trade.[46] Even a non-competition clause that is ancillary to an otherwise valid transaction or relationship[47] may be unreasonably in restraint of trade. Many states will not enforce noncompete agreements unless the provision is narrowly written to protect the employer's legiti-

---

[42] REST. (2d) CONTRACTS § 179(b)(i).

[43] *Heyde Companies, Inc. v. Dove Healthcare, LLC*, 654 N.W.2d 830 (Wisc. 2002).

[44] *Cohen v. Orthalliance New Image, Inc.*, 252 F.Supp.2d 761 (N.D.Ind. 2003). On the application of the so-called "rule of reason" in determining whether a restraint is reasonable, and therefore enforceable, see REST. (2d) CONTRACTS § 186, comment a. *See, e.g., Dominic Wenzell, D.M.D. P.C. v. Ingrim*, 228 P.3d 103 (Alaska 2010) (holding that enforceability of covenant not to compete in contract for sale of dental practice required consideration of whether restriction was no greater than needed to protect goodwill in the business and whether purchaser's need to protect goodwill outweighed hardship to seller and likely injury to public); *Deutsch v. Barsky*, 795 A.2d 669 (D.C.App. 2002) (applying similar considerations as to mutual covenant not to compete in dispute between former partners in dental practice). *Cf. Reliable Fire Equipment Co. v. Arredondo*, 965 N.E.2d 393 (Ill. 2011) (applying similar considerations in reviewing noncompetition restrictive covenants in employment agreements); *Schmersahl, Treloar & Co., P.C. v. McHugh*, 28 S.W.3d 345 (Mo. App. 2000) (holding law firm nonsolicitation agreement unenforceable restrictive covenant in restraint of trade, because it did not seek to protect proprietary information or customer contacts but merely stability of plaintiff's workforce).

[45] On what constitutes a "non-ancillary restraint," see REST. (2d) CONTRACTS § 187, comment b. *Cf. Marsh USA Inc. v. Cook*, 354 S.W.3d 764 (Tex. 2011) (holding covenant not to compete was ancillary to otherwise enforceable employment agreement because business interest in goodwill being protected was reasonably related to stock options given to employee as consideration); *SKF USA, Inc. v. Bjerkness*, 636 F.Supp.2d 696 (N.D.Ill. 2009) (noting that restrictive covenants were enforceable if ancillary to valid contract or valid relationship, including at-will employment agreement); *Keller Corp. v. Kelley*, 187 P.3d 1133 (Colo. App. 2008) (holding that, although public policy generally did not favor covenants not to compete, agreement between franchisor and franchisee constituted agreement for purchase and sale of business, and covenant was reasonable as to its territorial reach and duration).

[46] REST. (2d) CONTRACTS § 187.

[47] For these purposes, a restraint that is "ancillary to a valid transaction or relationship" includes the following:

> (a) a promise by the seller of a business not to compete with the buyer in such a way as to injure the value of the business sold;
> (b) a promise by an employee or other agent not to compete with his employer or other principal;
> (c) a promise by a partner not to compete with the partnership.

REST. (2d) CONTRACTS § 188(2)(a)-(c).

mate interests[48] and does not cause undue hardship to the employee or otherwise injure the public.[49]

3. Family Law and Policy

Family law is another important source of public policies that may influence contract interpretation. Courts may derive constraints on the enforcement of promises or other contract terms from the need to prevent "impairment of family relations."[50] So, for example, a promise that unreasonably restrains a person's right to marry is unenforceable on grounds of public policy.[51] A promise by a married person or by a person contemplating marriage that changes some essential incident of the marital relationship[52] in a way detrimental to the public interest – such as forcing the person to leave the marital home at a moment's notice from the spouse or intended spouse, even upon an agreed-upon payment – would be unenforceable on grounds of public policy.[53] Likewise, a separation agreement may be unenforceable on grounds of public policy unless it is made *after* separation or in contemplation of an *immediate* separation and is fair under the circumstances.[54] Finally, a promise that unreasonably encouraged divorce or separation – for example, a promise to pay a spouse a large sum of money in return for the spouse's promise to obtain a divorce[55] – would be unenforceable on grounds of public policy.[56]

---

[48] On narrowing the restriction in light of the employer's legitimate interests, see REST. (2d) CONTRACTS § 188, comment b. *Cf. Orca Communications Unlimited, LLC v. Noder*, 314 P.3d 89 (Ariz. App. 2013) (holding noncompete and customer nonsolicitation covenants contained in employment agreement to be broader than necessary to protect employer's legitimate business interests); *Reed Mill & Lumber Co., Inc. v. Jensen*, 165 P.3d 733 (Colo. App. 2007) (holding duration of noncompete agreement signed in connection with the sale of company unreasonable and unenforceable for additional three-year period after former employee had continued to work at company for six years after its sale to purchaser); *Freiburger v. J-U-B Engineers, Inc.*, 111 P.3d 100 (Idaho 2005) (holding covenant not to compete that prohibited former employee from providing any services to employer's clients, current, past, and potential, without regard to whether employee had had any contact with these clients, was an unreasonable, overbroad means of protecting employer's legitimate business interest in goodwill); *Statco Wireless, LLC v. Southwestern Bell Wireless, LLC,,* 95 S.W.3d 13 (Ark. App. 2003) (holding noncompete agreement, applying only to "key" employees and limited to one-year period, not overly broad).

[49] REST. (2d) CONTRACTS § 188(1)(a)-(b). On the harm to the promisor and injury to the public, see REST. (2d) CONTRACTS § 188, comment c.

[50] REST. (2d) CONTRACTS § 179(b)(ii).

[51] REST. (2d) CONTRACTS § 189.

[52] On the nature of a change in an essential incident of the marital relationship, see REST. (2d) CONTRACTS § 190, comment a.

[53] REST. (2d) CONTRACTS § 190(1).

[54] REST. (2d) CONTRACTS § 190(1).

[55] Presumably, this would not include an offer that "[f]or two cents, I'd walk out right now." *Cf.* REST. (2d) CONTRACTS § 190, Illus. 3 (involving promise to pay $50,000 if spouse agrees to obtain divorce).

[56] REST. (2d) CONTRACTS § 190(2). *Cf. In re Marriage of Traster*, 291 P.3d 494 Kan. App. 2012) (upholding postmarital agreement that parties had signed during their marriage, where parties had been married for 25 years and husband did not file for divorce until three years after signing agreement in question; holding that no evidence supported trial court's finding that agreement created substantial incentive for husband to file for divorce as soon as possible); *Black v. Powers*, 628 S.E.2d 546 (Va. App. 2006) (upholding parties' prenuptial agreement).

Provisions in a prenuptial agreement purporting to limit or waive spousal support in the event of divorce have been held to be void as contrary to public policy, and could be severed from valid portions of such an agreement.[57] Likewise, an agreed stipulation and order modifying a decree of divorce providing that neither party would seek modification of child support would not estop a parent from contesting enforceability of the stipulation as a contract provision invalidated by applicable public policy.[58] Similarly, an agreement affecting custody of a minor child is unenforceable on grounds of public policy unless its provisions are "consistent with the best interest of the child."[59]

4. Other Protected Interests

The risk that a contract provision might interfere with other protected interests remains a continuing concern for public policy.[60] One manifestation of this concern is the use of unconscionability as a policing device in contracts law,[61] as reflected in UCC § 2-302.[62] Another is the rule that "[a] promise to commit a tort or to induce the commission of a tort is unenforceable on grounds of public policy."[63] In addition, a promise to violate

---

[57] *Sanford v. Sanford*, 694 N.W.2d 283 (S.D. 2005).

[58] *Fernandez v. Fernandez*, 222 P.3d 1031 (Nev. 2010).

[59] REST. (2d) CONTRACTS § 191.

[60] REST. (2d) CONTRACTS § 179(b)(iii).

[61] *See, e.g., Parilla v. IAP Worldwide Services VI, Inc.*, 368 F.3d 269 (3d Cir. 2004) (holding that provision in employment contract that each party bears his or her own costs, expenses, and attorney's fees, was unconscionable, when viewed as of time contract was made); *Kinkel v. Cingular Wireless LLC*, 857 N.E.2d 250 (Ill. 2006) (in class action by cellular-telephone customers challenging early-termination fee as illegal penalty, holding arbitration clause of service contract enforceable, but holding class-action waiver clause prohibiting class arbitration unconscionable and unenforceable); *Swain v. Auto Services, Inc.*, 128 S.W.3d 103 (Mo. App. 2003) (holding venue provision of vehicle service contract to be unenforceable as unconscionable; severing from general agreement to arbitrate)..

[62] This policing function, and its conceptual affinity to public policy constraints is made explicit in the official comments to § 2-302:

> This section is intended to make it possible for the courts to police explicitly against the contracts or clauses which they find to be unconscionable. *In the past such policing has been accomplished* by adverse construction of language, by manipulation of the rules of offer and acceptance or *by determinations that the clause is contrary to public policy* or to the dominant purpose of the contract.

UCC § 2-302, Official Comment 1 (emphasis added).

[63] REST. (2d) CONTRACTS § 192. *See, e.g., Fisher v. Halliburton*, 696 F.Supp.2d 710 (S.D.Tex. 2010) (holding that government contractor is not immune with respect to claims of fraud, assault-and-battery, and negligence by civilian employees since alleged conduct exceeded authority of government contract). *Cf.* REST. (2d) CONTRACTS § 194 (promise that tortiously interferes with performance of contract with third person or tortiously induces promise to commit breach of contract unenforceable on grounds of public policy); REST. (2d) CONTRACTS § 195(1) (contract term exempting party from tort liability for harm caused intentionally or recklessly unenforceable on grounds of public policy). For similar public policy constraints on contract term exempting party from negligence liability under certain circumstances and on certain terms exempting party from products liability, see REST. (2d) CONTRACTS § 195(2)-(3). *See, e.g., Brooten v. Hickok Rehabilitation Services, LLC*, 831 N.W.2d 445 (Wisc. App. 2013) (holding that exculpatory waiver in health

a fiduciary duty, or to induce such a violation, would be unenforceable on grounds of public policy.[64] Similarly, a contract term "unreasonably exempting a party from the legal consequences of a misrepresentation is unenforceable."[65]

"One of the most frequent applications" of public policy constraints[66] involves the situation where conduct of a business activity or participation in a trade is subject to a licensing, registration or similar requirement.[67] Failure to comply with the requirement would render a promise in consideration of the conduct or participation[68] unenforceable on grounds of public policy if "(a) the requirement has a regulatory purpose,[69] and (b) the interest in the enforcement of the promise is clearly outweighed by the public policy behind the requirement."[70]

Another example would be laws regulating the conduct of professional activity, under which fee-sharing with unregulated non-professionals is prohibited. An agreement providing for such fee-sharing may be unenforceable as against public policy.[71] Likewise,

---

club agreement was unenforceable because it was impermissibly broad and all-inclusive); *Rhino riFund, LLLP v. Hutchins*, 215 P.3d 1186 (Colo. App. 2009) (holding exculpatory provision in agreement between investor and investment fund unenforceable to extent it purported to exempt manager from personal tort liability, where manager's actions were intentional, unauthorized, and self-serving); *Airfreight Exp. Ltd v. Evergreen Air Center, Inc.*, 158 P.3d 232 (Ariz. App. 2007) (involving limitation-of-damages clause); *Gavin v. YMCA of Metropolitan Los Angeles*, 106 Cal.App.4th 662, 669, 131 Cal.Rptr.2d 168 (Cal. App. 2003) (holding agreement exculpating child-care provider from its own negligence void as against public policy).

[64] REST. (2d) CONTRACTS § 193. *See, e.g., Omnicare, Inc. v. NCS Healthcare, Inc.*, 818 A.2d 914 (Del. 2003) (holding that defensive measures to protect merger transaction were unenforceable because they were preclusive, coercive, and invalid as applied; merger agreement provision requiring board of directors to submit merger transaction for stockholder vote prevented board from exercising business judgment and discharging fiduciary duties to minority stockholders).

[65] REST. (2d) CONTRACTS § 196.

[66] REST. (2d) CONTRACTS § 181, comment a.

[67] *See, e.g., Marker & Associates, Inc. v. J. Allan Hall & Associates*, 314 F.Supp.2d 555 (E.D.N.C. 2004) (applying predecessor of § 181 to hold contract right of unlicensed reinsurance intermediary unenforceable).

[68] In other words, in the present context we are dealing with the right of the *non-complying party* to enforce the other party's promise. REST. (2d) CONTRACTS § 181, comment d. Enforceability of the non-complying party's promise by the *other party* is governed by the general rule stated in REST. (2d) CONTRACTS § 178. *See* text and accompanying notes 21-35 (discussing § 178). *See also Vanguard Const. & Development Co., Inc. v. Polsky*, 24 Misc.3d 854, 879 N.Y.S.2d 300 (N.Y. Sup.Ct. 2009) (holding that, while unlicensed home improvement contractor's rights under construction contract were unenforceable as a matter of public policy, homeowners rights under contract were enforceable).

[69] *See* REST. (2d) CONTRACTS § 181, comment b (discussing "regulatory purpose" and its role in decision whether to impose public policy constraint).

[70] REST. (2d) CONTRACTS § 181(a)-(b). For discussion of balancing of the interest in enforcement and constraining public policy, see REST. (2d) CONTRACTS § 181, comment c. *See also MGM Const. Services Corp. v. Travelers Cas. & Sur. Co. of America*, 57 So.3d 884 (Fla. App. 2011) (holding that material questions existed as to whether public policy behind subcontractor licensing ordinance clearly outweighed interest in allowing subcontractor to enforce contractor's promise).

[71] *Martello v. Santana*, 713 F.3d 309 (6th Cir. 2013) (holding contracts between attorney and doctor, for certain medical/legal consulting work by doctor. unenforceable under rules prohibiting fee-sharing); *Mason v. Orthodontic Centers of Colorado, Inc.*, 516 F.Supp.2d 1205 (D.Colo. 2007) (invalidating fee-sharing agreement between dentist and office management company). *But cf. Ritacca v. Girardi*, 996 N.E.2d 236 (Ill. App. 2013) (holding that public policy against medical fee-

regulatory programs that restrict entry into and the conduct of certain business activity are a source of public policy constraints, activities such as operation of a bar or other business serving or selling alcoholic beverages[72] or participation in the construction trade.[73]

Foreign policy constraints, such as international economic sanctions, is another frequent source of public policy concern.[74] Contracts for international trade in goods or for transborder provision of services may be unenforceable if they involve trading with nationals of an enemy nation, or involve transactions prohibited by governmental sanctions against a target country or its nationals.[75]

III. LABOR'S LOVE LOST

West Bestie International, the nationwide hotel chain, has had a series of collective bargaining agreements with the United Steel, Paper and Forestry, Rubber, Manufacturing, Energy, Allied Industrial and Service Workers International Union, AFL–CIO–CLC or its predecessor unions (hereinafter referred to as "the Union") for 30 years. The Union represents the hotel and restaurant workers employed by West Bestie, consistent with the federal Labor Management Relations Act (LMRA) and the Employee Retirement Income Security Act (ERISA). Three years ago, West Bestie entered into a master collective-bargaining agreement and a Pension, Insurance, and Service Award Agreement (P & I agreement) with the Union, generally similar to agreements the Union had negotiated

---

splitting agreements did not clearly outweigh the interest in enforcing settlement agreement to dissolve medical practice); *Burnison v. Johnston*, 277 Neb. 622, 764 N.W.2d 96 (Neb. 2009) (holding that assignment of legal fees owed for previous services not barred as against public policy); *Kepple and Co., Inc. v. Cardiac, Thoracic and Endovascular Therapies, S.C.*, 920 N.E.2d 1189 (Ill. App. 2009) (holding fee-sharing clause unenforceable and essential part of medical billing and collection contract; holding remaining provisions of contract not severable and therefore void and unenforceable).

[72] *See, e.g., Parente v. Pirozzoli*, 866 A.2d 629 (Conn. App. 2005) (holding partnership agreement for ownership and operation of bar by former owner and new owner, who had a felony conviction, illegal as contrary to public policy and therefore unenforceable); *Zenon v. R.E. Yeagher Management Corporation*, 748 A.2d 900 (Conn. App. 2000) (holding promissory note unenforceable, because its execution was integral to illegal transfer of lessor's liquor license to lessees).

[73] *See, e.g., Austin Bldg. Co. v. Rago, Ltd.*, 63 So.3d 31 (Fla. App. 2011) (holding that whether general contractor was properly licensed at time subcontractor began working on project was necessary issue in determining whether construction contract was unenforceable). *But cf. K. Miller Const. Co., Inc. v. McGinnis*, 938 N.E.2d 471 (Ill. 2010) (holding that state statute requiring contracts for remodeling work over $1,000 to be in writing did not render oral contract unenforceable).

[74] *See generally* MICHAEL P. MALLOY, UNITED STATES ECONOMIC SANCTIONS: THEORY AND PRACTICE (Kluwer Law International: 2001) (analyzing and discussing international economic sanctions law and policy).

[75] *See, e.g., Kashani v. Tsann Kuen China Enterprise Co., Ltd.*, 118 Cal.App.4th 531, 13 Cal.Rptr.3d 174 (Cal. App. 2004) (holding that plaintiffs could not legally establish breach of contract claim, because contract with Chinese, Taiwanese, and American corporations to build manufacturing plant in Iran for production of computer products was illegal and against public policy, pursuant to executive orders and federal regulations prohibiting trade with Iran without a license).

with West Bestie and other hotel companies in the past. Among other things, the master agreement provided that the company would provide low-rate, 30-year residential mortgage financing for qualified employees, as follows:

> The Company agrees that it will provide residential mortgage financing for any qualified employee with a minimum of ten (10) years of continuous service, the mortgage to be for a term at signing of 30 years at an annual rate of interest set at two percentage points below the average annual percentage rate on mortgages guaranteed by the Federal National Mortgage Association or the Federal Home Loan Mortgage Corporation. To qualify for this program, an employee (1) must be lawfully married under the laws of the state of residence of the employee; (2) must be either a member of an under-served minority or a non-male; and, (3) must provide documentation, as required by the Company Benefit Office, of the employee's status under criteria (1) – (2) above. Failure to provide the required documentation as specified by the Company Benefit Office shall constitute grounds for denial of any application. The Company agrees that all mortgage documents and related disclosures, notices, and other mortgage-related documents shall be made available to the employee in digital form only, and shall be available to the employee at a website established by the Company for these purposes.

The P & I agreement provided for retiree health care benefits as follows:

> Employees who retire on or after January 1, 1996 and who are eligible for and receiving a monthly pension under the 1993 Pension Plan . . . whose full years of attained age and full years of attained continuous service . . . at the time of retirement equals 95 or more points will receive a full Company contribution towards the cost of health care benefits provided under the agreement. . . . Employees who have less than 95 points at the time of retirement will receive a reduced Company contribution. The Company contribution will be reduced by 2% for every point less than 95. Employees will be required to pay the balance of the health care contribution, as estimated by the Company annually in advance, for the [health care] benefits. Failure to pay the required medical contribution will result in cancellation of coverage.
>
> As of the effective date, and for the duration of this Agreement thereafter, the Employer will provide the following program of hospital benefits, hospital-medical benefits, surgical benefits and prescription drug benefits for eligible employees and their dependents. . . .

The P & I agreement provided for renegotiation of its terms in three years.

Questions.

A. After finding a small, charming bungalow close to the beach for sale at a very reasonable price, Whittington J. White contacted the West Bestie Benefits Office to inquire about applying for a discounted 30-year mortgage. Whit has worked as the night clerk for a West Bestie Resort Hotel for eleven years. Unfortunately, the Benefits Office told Whit that, even though he had sufficient years of service, he was not qualified for the mortgage program. Whit is not married, and he is neither a member of an under-served minority nor a non-male.

Whit was furious when he was turned down for the mortgage. "I put in my time," Whit explained to you, "I should be able to get a mortgage. It's grossly unfair." You weren't sure about that, until you came across the Equal Credit Opportunity Act regulations of the Consumer Financial Protection Bureau,[76] excerpted below. After you have reviewed these regulations, consider the following questions.

1. Is West Bestie's residential mortgage program consistent with the requirements of the CFPB regulations?

2. If the program is not in compliance with the regulations, would that mean that the collective bargaining agreement is unenforceable as against public policy?

3. Is there any way that you could thread through these facts and come up with a legal argument that would explain why Whit should be entitled to a mortgage under the collective bargaining agreement?

Code of Federal Regulations
Title 12. Banks and Banking
Chapter X. Bureau of Consumer Financial Protection
Part 1002. Equal Credit Opportunity Act (Regulation B)

12 C.F.R. § 1002.4
§ 1002.4 General rules.
(a) Discrimination. A creditor shall not discriminate against an applicant on a prohibited basis regarding any aspect of a credit transaction.

(b) Discouragement. A creditor shall not make any oral or written statement, in advertising or otherwise, to applicants or prospective applicants that would discourage on a prohibited basis a reasonable person from making or pursuing an application. . . .

(d) Form of disclosures—
(1) General rule. A creditor that provides in writing any disclosures or information required by this part must provide the disclosures in a clear and conspicuous manner and, except for the disclosures required by §§ 1002.5 . . . , in a form the applicant may retain.
(2) Disclosures in electronic form. The disclosures required by this part that are required to be given in writing may be provided to the applicant in electronic form, subject to . . . consumer consent. . . .

---

[76] For background information about the CFPB, see 1 MICHAEL P. MALLOY, BANKING LAW AND REGULATION § 1C.10[E] (2d ed. 2011).

12 C.F.R. § 1002.5
§ 1002.5 Rules concerning requests for information.

(a) General rules—
(1) Requests for information. Except as provided in paragraphs (b) through (d) of this section, a creditor may request any information in connection with a credit transaction. This paragraph does not limit or abrogate any Federal or state law regarding privacy, privileged information, credit reporting limitations, or similar restrictions on obtainable information. . . .

(b) Limitation on information about race, color, religion, national origin, or sex. A creditor shall not inquire about the race, color, religion, national origin, or sex of an applicant or any other person in connection with a credit transaction, except as provided in paragraphs (b)(1) and (b)(2) of this section.
(1) Self-test. A creditor may inquire about the race, color, religion, national origin, or sex of an applicant or any other person in connection with a credit transaction for the purpose of conducting a self-test [of compliance with the Equal Credit Opportunity Act]. A creditor that makes such an inquiry shall disclose orally or in writing, at the time the information is requested, that:
(i) The applicant will not be required to provide the information;
(ii) The creditor is requesting the information to monitor its compliance with the Federal Equal Credit Opportunity Act;
(iii) Federal law prohibits the creditor from discriminating on the basis of this information, or on the basis of an applicant's decision not to furnish the information; and
(iv) If applicable, certain information will be collected based on visual observation or surname if not provided by the applicant or other person.
(2) Sex. An applicant may be requested to designate a title on an application form (such as Ms., Miss, Mr., or Mrs.) if the form discloses that the designation of a title is optional. An application form shall otherwise use only terms that are neutral as to sex.

(c) Information about a spouse or former spouse—
(1) General rule. Except as permitted in this paragraph, a creditor may not request any information concerning the spouse or former spouse of an applicant.
(2) Permissible inquiries. A creditor may request any information concerning an applicant's spouse (or former spouse under paragraph (c)(2)(v) of this section) that may be requested about the applicant if:
(i) The spouse will be permitted to use the account;
(ii) The spouse will be contractually liable on the account;
(iii) The applicant is relying on the spouse's income as a basis for repayment of the credit requested;
(iv) The applicant resides in a community property state or is relying on property located in such a state as a basis for repayment of the credit requested; or
(v) The applicant is relying on alimony, child support, or separate maintenance payments from a spouse or former spouse as a basis for repayment of the credit requested.
(3) Other accounts of the applicant. A creditor may request that an applicant list any account on which the applicant is contractually liable and to provide the name and address of the person in whose name the account is held. A creditor may also ask an applicant to list the names in which the applicant has previously received credit.

(d) Other limitations on information requests—
(1) Marital status. If an applicant applies for individual unsecured credit, a creditor shall not inquire about the applicant's marital status unless the applicant resides in a community property state or is relying on property located in such a state as a basis for repayment of the credit requested. If an application is for other than individual unsecured credit, a creditor may inquire about the applicant's marital status, but shall use only the terms married, unmarried, and separated. A creditor may explain that the category unmarried includes single, divorced, and widowed persons.
(2) Disclosure about income from alimony, child support, or separate maintenance. A creditor shall not inquire whether income stated in an application is derived from alimony, child support, or separate maintenance payments unless the creditor discloses to the applicant that such income need not be revealed if the applicant does not want the creditor to consider it in determining the applicant's creditworthiness.

(3) Childbearing, childrearing. A creditor shall not inquire about birth control practices, intentions concerning the bearing or rearing of children, or capability to bear children. A creditor may inquire about the number and ages of an applicant's dependents or about dependent-related financial obligations or expenditures, provided such information is requested without regard to sex, marital status, or any other prohibited basis.

(e) Permanent residency and immigration status. A creditor may inquire about the permanent residency and immigration status of an applicant or any other person in connection with a credit transaction. . . .

12 C.F.R. § 1002.7
§ 1002.7 Rules concerning extensions of credit.

(a) Individual accounts. A creditor shall not refuse to grant an individual account to a creditworthy applicant on the basis of sex, marital status, or any other prohibited basis.

(b) Designation of name. A creditor shall not refuse to allow an applicant to open or maintain an account in a birth-given first name and a surname that is the applicant's birth-given surname, the spouse's surname, or a combined surname. . . .

(d) Signature of spouse or other person—
(1) Rule for qualified applicant. Except as provided in this paragraph, a creditor shall not require the signature of an applicant's spouse or other person, other than a joint applicant, on any credit instrument if the applicant qualifies under the creditor's standards of creditworthiness for the amount and terms of the credit requested. A creditor shall not deem the submission of a joint financial statement or other evidence of jointly held assets as an application for joint credit. . . .

B. Assume that on the expiration of the last collective bargaining agreement, West Bestie announced that it would begin requiring retirees to contribute to the cost of their health care benefits. Whit's father, a recent retiree after 30 years with West Bestie, thinks that this decision is "a betrayal of WB obligations to us old fellows. We bargained for lifetime contribution-free health care benefits for us, our surviving spouses, and our kids, and that's what WB promised us."

1. Is Whit Sr. correct? Does it make a difference that the agreement was likely to be renegotiated every three years or so?

2. Is this dispute governed by ordinary contract law, or should it be governed by regulatory principles under federal labor law? If, arguably those principles are intended to give legal validity to agreements negotiated by a union *on behalf of* its members, should we assume that as a matter of public policy the agreement should be interpreted more broadly than the strict language of the agreement might otherwise suggest?

3. Would it be reasonable to argue that parties to collective bargaining would intend retiree benefits to vest for life because such benefits are typically understood as a form of delayed compensation or reward for past services?

C. Are the following contract promises enforceable or unenforceable on the grounds of public policy?

1.   1. *A* promises to pay *B* $100 if the Wonelles win their intramural handball match with the Tortfeasors, and *B* promises to pay *A* $100 if the Tortfeasors win – jointly or severally. A state statute in the state where their law school is located makes wagering a crime and makes a promise in relation to a wager or game of chance "void."

☐ Enforceable

☐ Unenforceable

2. *A* and *B* agree that *A* will sell and *B* will buy, at a fixed price per bushel, one thousand bushels of kidneys of the *Helix pomatia*, delivery at any time that *A* chooses during the next 30 days. Because of the difficulty of finding and harvesting *Helix pomatia*, *A* says "this is like a race to the finish line."

☐ Enforceable

☐ Unenforceable

3. In order to finance his *Helix pomatia* business, *A* borrows $10,000 from the *C* National Bank, promising to repay it with interest at the rate of twelve per cent. A state statute in the state where *A* operates fixes the maximum legal rate of interest on such loans at seven per cent, and it provides that a promise to pay a greater sum renders the entire loan agreement "null and void" as usurious. A federal statute applicable to national banks also fixes the maximum legal rate of interest on such loans at seven per cent, but provides that a promise to pay a greater sum is "void" as to all of the promised interest but not as to the principal.

a. As to the promise to pay 12 percent interest on the loan?

☐ Enforceable

☐ Unenforceable

b. As to the loan agreement as a whole?

☐ Enforceable

☐ Unenforceable

4. *A* and *B* agree that *A* will sell and *B* will buy, at a fixed price per bushel, one thousand bushels of kidneys of the *Helix pomatia* to be delivered by *A* in his own truck at a designated time and place. A municipal parking ordinance makes unloading of a truck at that time and place an offense punishable by a fine of up to $50.

a. As to the delivery terms of the contract?

☐ Enforceable

☐ Unenforceable

b. As to the sales contract a whole?

☐ Enforceable

☐ Unenforceable

5. *E*, the operator of a website ConsumerDude.com, promises *A* that he will post an unfavorable review about *A*'s competitor Gastropoddies, although both *A* and *E* know that some of the statements in the review are false and defamatory, if *A* pays *E* $500. *A* has paid the $500.

☐Enforceable

☐Unenforceable

6. *F*, the owner of Gastropoddies, promises to pay *E* $1,000 if ConsumerDude will post a statement that *A*'s *Helix pomatia* are actually *Lissachatina fulica*, a statement that both *E* and *F* know to be false and likely to damage *A*'s business substantially. *E* has posted the statement.

☐Enforceable

☐Unenforceable

7. *F* promises to transfer to *E* an autographed photo of Sonny Tufts, a collectible worth $11,000, if *E* pays *F* $1,000 and posts on ConsumerDude.com a statement that *A*'s *Helix pomatia* are actually *Lissachatina fulica*, a statement that both *E* and *F* know to be false and likely to damage *A*'s business substantially. *E* pays *F* $1,000 and posts the statement.

☐Enforceable

☐Unenforceable

8. *A* promises to pay *F* $10,000 if *F* will refrain from competing with him for a year.

☐Enforceable

☐Unenforceable

9. *A* concludes an agreement to sell large quantities of *Helix pomatia* to *G* by bribing *G*'s purchasing agent, and *G* agrees to pay a substantial price for the goods. *A* delivers the goods to *G*.

☐Enforceable

☐Unenforceable

TABLE OF CASES

References are to page numbers of this text.

INDEX

References are to page numbers of this text.